Church

"Living Church" Series
J. Dwight Stinnett, series editor

Available now...
Empowering Laity, Engaging Leaders
Tapping the Root for Ministry
Susan E. Gillies and M. Ingrid Dvirnak

Caring Pastors, Caring People
Equipping Your Church for Pastoral Care
Marvin A. McMickle

Making Friends, Making Disciples
Growing Your Church through Authentic Relationships
Lee B. Spitzer

Coming in Spring 2013...
Learning Mission, Living Mission: Churches That Work

www.judsonpress.com / 800-4-JUDSON

Empowering Laity, Engaging Leaders

Tapping the Root for Ministry

SUSAN E. GILLIES AND M. INGRID DVIRNAK

J. DWIGHT STINNETT, SERIES EDITOR

Living Church

JUDSON PRESS
PUBLISHERS SINCE 1824

Join our mailing list for updates and special offers.
www.judsonpress.com/mailing_list.cfm

Empowering Laity, Engaging Leaders: Tapping the Root for Ministry
© 2012 by Judson Press, Valley Forge, PA 19482-0851
All rights reserved.

The stories in this book are based on actual people and churches, but in most cases names and identifying features have been changed to protect the privacy of the individuals and congregations.

Judson Press has made every effort to trace the ownership of all quotes. In the event of a question arising from the use of a quote, we regret any error made and will be pleased to make the necessary correction in future printings and editions of this book.

Scripture quotations marked CEV are taken from the Contemporary English Version, copyright © 1991, 1992, 1995 by American Bible Society. Used by permission.

Scripture quotations marked MSG are taken from *The Message*. Copyright 1993, 1994, 1995, 1996, 2000, 2001, 2002. Used by permission of NavPress Publishing Group.

Scripture quotations marked NEB are taken from *The New English Bible*. Copyright © The Delegates of the Oxford University Press and the Syndics of the Cambridge University Press 1961, 1970. Reprinted by permission.

Scripture quotations marked NIV are taken from the Holy Bible, *New International Version®, NIV®*. Copyright © 1973, 1978, 1984, 2011 by Biblica, Inc.™ Used by permission. All rights reserved worldwide.

Scripture quotations marked NRSV are taken from the *New Revised Standard Version of the Bible*, copyrighted 1989 by the Division of Christian Education of the National Council of Churches of Christ in the United States of America, and are used by permission. All rights reserved.

Scripture quotations marked TEV are from the Today's English Version—Second Edition Copyright © 1992 by American Bible Society. Used by permission.

Interior design by Wendy Ronga, Hampton Design Group. www.hamptondesigngroup.com
Cover design by Tobias Becker and Birdbox Graphic Design. www.birdboxdesign.com.

Library of Congress Cataloging-in-Publication Data
Gillies, Susan E. Empowering laity, engaging leaders: tapping the root for ministry/Susan E. Gillies and M. Ingrid Dvirnak.—1st ed. p. cm.—(Living church) Includes bibliographical references (p.). ISBN 978-0-8170-1710-1 (pbk.: alk. paper) 1. Christian leadership. 2. Laity. I. Dvirnak, M. Ingrid. II. Title. BV652.1.G55 2012
253—dc23   2012003657

Printed in the U.S.A.
First Edition, 2012.

To three wise men
who helped churches
find new life through
empowered lay leadership:
Richard Sutton,
Wayne Dvirnak,
William Diehl

Contents

Preface to the Series

Living
Church

"What happened? Just a few years ago we were a strong church. We had thriving ministries and supported a worldwide mission effort. Our community knew us and cared about what we did. Now we're not sure if we can survive another year."

It is a painful conversation I have had with more church leaders than I can name here.

I explained how images such as *meltdown*, *tsunami*, *earthquake*, and *storm* have been used to describe the crisis developing in the North American church over the last twenty-five years. Our present crisis is underscored by the American Religious Identification Survey 2008. Not just one local congregation, but nearly every church is being swamped by the changes.

Volumes have already been written in analysis of the current situation and in critique of the church. I suggested a few books and workshops that I knew, trying to avoid the highly technical works. But the church leader with whom I was talking was overwhelmed by all the analysis. "Yes, I am sure that is true. But what do we do? When I look at what is happening and I hear all the criticism, I wonder if the church has a future at all. Do we deserve one?"

I emphasized that there are no simple answers and that those who offer simplistic solutions are either deceived or deceiving. There is no "church cookbook" for today (and I'm not sure there ever really was one). I tried to avoid an equally simplistic pietistic answer.

Still, the church leader pressed. "So is the church dead? Do we just need to schedule a funeral and get over it? We are all so tired and frustrated."

I do not accept the sentiment of futility and despair about the future of the church. I believe the church is alive and persists not because of what we do, but because of what God has done and continues to do in the church.

The pain is real, however, as are the struggle and the longing. I wanted to help church leaders such as this one understand, but not be overwhelmed by the peculiar set of forces impacting the church today. But information was not enough. I wanted to encourage them with specific things that can be done, without implying that success is guaranteed or that human effort is sufficient. I wanted them to learn from what others are doing, not to copy them mechanically, but to use what others are doing as eyeglasses to look closely at their own context. I wanted them to avoid all the churchy labels that are out there and be a living church in their community, empowered and sustained by the living God.

Those of us who work with groups of churches and who pay attention to the things that are happening around us know that several forces are having a devastating affect on the church today. Both formal studies and personal observation identify at least eight key areas where the impact has been especially acute.

These areas are biblical illiteracy, financial pressures, overwhelming diversity, shrinking numbers, declining leadership base, brokenness in and around us, narrowing inward focus, and unraveling of spiritual community. It is not hard to see how each of these is related to the others.

Living Church is a series from Judson Press intended to address each of these forces from a congregational perspective. While our authors are well-informed biblically, theologically, and topically, these volumes are not intended to be an exercise in ecclesiastical academics. Our intent is to empower congregational leaders (both clergy and laity) to rise to the challenge before us.

Our goal is not merely to lament our state of crisis, but to identify creative and constructive strategies for our time and place so that we can move on to effective responses. Our time and place is the American church in the twenty-first century.

The first volume in this series, *Making Friends, Making Disciples*, by Dr. Lee Spitzer, addresses the issue of shrinking numbers by reminding us of the spiritual discipline of being and making friends, not with some ulterior motive, but because God has called us to relationship.

The second volume, *Caring Pastors, Caring People*, by Dr. Marvin McMickle, confronts the growing brokenness within and around the church by challenging pastors and laity who will reach out to provide pastoral care first to one another within the congregation and then for the community outside the doors of the church.

In this third volume, *Empowering Laity, Engaging Leaders: Tapping the Root for Ministry*, Susan Gillies and Ingrid Dvirnak consider the declining leadership base experienced in many churches today. The focus and direction of this book are evident in the first sentence of the Introduction: "Church vitality depends on the involvement of both clergy and laity in meaningful ministry."

With an easy, conversational style Gillies and Dvirnak identify the obstacles to cultivating lay leadership. They suggest that the primary reason for growing disengagement among church members is disillusionment. But Susan and Ingrid do not stop with the painful critique. They go on to suggest ways over, around, and through these obstacles, beginning with establishing greater clarity and consistency in church structure and purpose. Their goal is to "create an environment in which leaders and followers can actually *be* the church—the Body of Christ."

This volume makes a few points that deserve special emphasis. First, there is value (both to the church and to the individual) in having leaders rotate through a season of followership—when they step out of a leadership role and follow someone else for a while. Second, the authors emphasize that "effective leadership demands personal wholeness"—and that means leaders must cultivate spiritual health in themselves. Third, the process of leadership development begins with children and extends through retirees. No one is too young or too old to be equipped for and engaged in leadership.

Gillies and Dvirnak are clear: "Engaging laity takes work. Identification and cultivation of leaders is an ongoing, intentional process." They draw strongly on the image of the church described in Ephesians 4:1-13 in calling pastors and other church leaders to do that work. This volume will be an invaluable tool in equipping today's leaders to identify and train new leaders for tomorrow— leaders who are crucial for the future of vital churches that are doing Christ's transforming work in the world.

Rev. Dr. J. Dwight Stinnett
Series Editor
Executive Minister
American Baptist Churches,
Great Rivers Region

Acknowledgments

We are grateful for the churches, pastors, and leaders who planted seeds and encouraged us along each step of our life journeys. Both of us have experienced "church" in a variety of settings across the United States. In each place, we have learned essential lessons and have had opportunities to put them into practice.

In the writing of this book, we owe a special debt of gratitude to Kathy Brown, David Lundholm, Paul Marine, Harry Riggs, Robin Stoops, Carol Sutton, Bernice Vincent, Aidsand F. Wright-Riggins III. Our series editor, Dwight Stinnett, provided unceasing encouragement from the outset. Our publisher, Laura Alden, and our editor, Rebecca Irwin-Diehl, provided valuable guidance all along the way.

Where Have All the Leaders Gone?

Church vitality depends on the involvement of both clergy and laity in meaningful ministry. However, quality lay leadership in local churches seems to be vanishing. Many church members are finding themselves less and less engaged in the ministry of the local church. The attraction of being part of an entertained audience doesn't seem to be enough. Still others are overengaged, filling positions for the sake of keeping the institution afloat. They are busy but find themselves unfulfilled with little sense that they are the hands and feet of Jesus.

Little by little, across the country, seeds of new life are sprouting in a growing number of churches that have been essentially dormant. Pastors and members are beginning to find that focusing outward instead of inward is tremendously rewarding, more fitting of a gospel people, and not as difficult as they feared. Instead of being critical of churches that seem more successful, these churches are no longer wasting time on comparisons. They are finding their own unique ways to reach out as the body of Christ.

These signs of new life can transform the negativity that has been so damaging to some churches. One cynic observed the role of laity in the church to be that of "pew fodder" for the institution. Somebody has to sit in the pew and put money in the offering plate in order to make the operation work. If the laity will just come and sit and pay, clergy will have a paycheck and a lovely church build-ing. Likewise, if the local church sends the money up the denomina-tional ladder, church bureaucrats will have steady income. The signs of new life, however, are changing cynicism to hope. Once-stagnant churches are beginning to learn how to become "engaged" commu-nities where clergy and laity minister together as the body of Christ.

Church life is impacted by three primary groups: the clergy who are the spiritual guides of the congregation; laity who are the mem-bers and visitors, some providing significant leadership within the congregation and some attending only occasionally; and an often overlooked group—the external faith leaders, the authors, speak-ers, denominational and seminary staff, and parachurch leaders who also inform the discussion on the role of the church and pro-vide resources for local church leaders.

Generally, institutions don't like being shaken up, but that's exactly what happens when laity, pastors, or external faith leaders decide they want to be bona fide parts of the body of Christ. The boat begins to rock. The very nature of institutions requires that they maintain the status quo. Their leaders must do everything in their power to smooth the waters and keep the boat from rocking. The problem with the church today is that in addition to internal challenges, the external culture has slammed the church with a tsunami of change. For many, the boat has not only rocked violent-ly, it has actually been torn apart. As a result, laity, pastors, and faith leaders find themselves floating next to each other, hanging on to broken pieces of the boat.

Another version of the story depicts faith leaders, pastors, and laity jumping ship when they realize their boat may come apart. In desperation, they find a supertanker (megachurch) that appears to offer safety in the midst of the turbulence. Inside the supertanker, the faith leader can quietly slip into anonymity. The pastor becomes all-important, and the laity—those paying pew sitters— have now simply morphed into movable chair sitters. When the tsunamis of cultural change hit, there appears to be little damage to the supertanker. The problem is that the tsunamis *have* caused damage. Cracks of doubt and restlessness have begun to appear deep within the bulkhead. Often the all-powerful leader begins to falter. This ship is not going to last either. What's next?

Actually, the tsunamis just keep coming. Many mainline churches have survived the first few tidal waves by hanging tight in the backwaters. But there are fewer and fewer places to hide. The boat is probably doomed from either the corrosion inside or the tsunamis outside. Who wants a leadership role under these circumstances?

Hope flies in the face of every calamity, however. Some ships have not yet capsized. Some are recoverable. Is there a way to rebuild the damaged boat and sail once again? Can we fashion one that will ride the waves better—a boat that is more suited to its original purpose? Will the emerging signs of new life give us the courage to craft new vessels or repair the old so we can rechart the voyage? How do we find the courage after the trauma we have experienced?

One way is to reframe what full leadership in the body of Christ looks like—the kind of leadership that will know how to guide a small boat or a supertanker. It isn't the size of the vessel that makes the difference—it's the leadership. In chapter 1, "Is This All There Is?," we examine what attracts people to a particular church and some of the disappointments leaders experience. In chapter 2, "Where Did Jesus Learn to Lead?," we consider key components of Jesus' leadership style. Chapter 3, "Amazing Ingredients for Action," addresses ways to identify and cultivate leaders. Chapter 4, "Christian Leaders on the Job," takes a look at ministry in the daily lives of Christian lay leaders. Chapter 5, "Linked Leadership," examines strategies for developing leaders, including children and youth. Chapter 6, "How Do I Make It Fit?," reviews personal wholeness as an essential component of successful leadership. Chapter 7, "Burden-Lifted Leadership," suggests steps for congregational wholeness that will lead to healthy, even joy-filled, leadership. Finally, chapter 8, "Practical Strategies for Engaging and Retaining Leaders," offers specific ideas for increasing the number and quality of lay leaders in local churches.

If you have picked up this book, you are probably aboard one of these threatened vessels. You may be a disheartened layperson, a disillusioned pastor, or a discouraged external faith leader, but you know you are called to share God's good news with others who inhabit your world. You're yearning for new insights into finding wholeness in your congregation. You want to know how to encourage leadership. You want to see signs of new life.

When Noah and his family had endured the rough waters of the great flood, a dove flew back to the ark with a freshly plucked olive leaf in its beak (Genesis 8:11, NRSV). That leaf was the symbol of new life for those "sailors." The waters had subsided at least enough for seeds to sprout and grow. That leaf heralded hope and possibility.

Regardless of where you find yourself in these turbulent days, something is growing that you may not yet see. The voyage to new life is not to be missed!

CHAPTER 1

Is This All There Is?

Taproots and the Church: A Look at the Botanical Metaphor
The taproot is the first root many seedlings put down when they
germinate. These conical core roots are somewhat enlarged and
primarily straight in form. They narrow as they grow
vertically downward. Lateral roots sprout from the
taproot. It is through these lateral roots that the taproot
gathers nutrients and delivers them to the plant, thereby enabling it to flourish. Taproots provide strong
anchors for plants, storing food and water. As older
leaves wear out and die, the taproot drives new growth
from the center.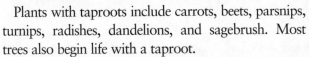

Plants with taproots include carrots, beets, parsnips,
turnips, radishes, dandelions, and sagebrush. Most
trees also begin life with a taproot.

What does the taproot have to do with the church? The church
is the people of God, most of whom are laity. A few emerge to
become anointed leaders whom we call clergy. But at the core, it is
the laity who constitute the body and provide strength for its ministry. The laity function as the taproot of the church. They gather
their nutrition from a host of sources both within and beyond the
church. The natural outcome is healthy fruit.

The resourceful laity in a Rocky Mountain church used their
individual gifts to create a unique children's ministry. Recognizing

that new children were attending Sunday church school, the adults determined to find additional ways to positively impact the lives of these children and their parents. "What do we have to offer?" they asked one another. As the brainstorming progressed, they found they had a great deal to offer. One woman knew how to decorate cakes and another was an artist. A man in the group was a ham radio operator; another was a photographer. Wood and leather crafters, tailors and needleworkers, cooks and bakers emerged. Together they decided to develop a children's ministry as a venue to pass along their passions as well as their faith.

Children learned new skills and developed relationships with their adult leaders. During the course of one evening a week, leaders shared their talents and personal faith stories. When children began bringing their friends, additional adults became involved. The news of this children's ministry spread quickly in the small town, and after several months, the church began to experience the fruit of this lay-led ministry. New families were engaging in the life and ministry of the church. Because the people who were roots of the church allowed themselves to be tapped for kingdom work, both children and adults experienced Christian growth and renewal.

Of course, that's the ideal. Unfortunately, today's church too often falls short of that goal. People who aren't engaged in fruitful ministry in their church may actually be searching for "something more." In this chapter, we'll look at some common obstacles to cultivating lay leadership, and we'll lay the foundation for addressing those challenges throughout the rest of the book.

The Lament of the Church

Years ago singer Peggy Lee had a hit song titled "Is That All There Is?" The lyrics express disappointment with events that should be uniquely memorable. As the musical story unfolds, we learn that nothing turns out to be special after all. In response, the singer asks the haunting question, "Is that all there is?" over and over throughout the song. This lament has also become the cry of too many people inside the church.

The mission fair is over; the exhibits have been dismantled. Next on the agenda is the regularly scheduled monthly mission committee meeting, during which the evaluation of the fair will take place. Is this all there is to the mission arm of my church?

Vacation Bible school is on the church calendar, just as it is every year. Recruiting teachers is always a challenge, but recruiting children seems to be easy. VBS is the church's annual outreach to the neighborhood children. However, the children and their families live nearby all year long. Is a weeklong educational program the only outreach ministry we have that focuses on the children in the neighborhood?

The deacon board meets monthly. In addition, the deacons prepare and serve Communion regularly. Most of them make nursing home and hospital visits too. Yet some of them ask, "Is this all there is to being a spiritual leader in my church?"

Trustees take excellent care of the church building, but they may fail to differentiate between the church building and the church as the body of Christ. Is being a trustee only about paint and plaster, or is there a spiritual dynamic to being an overseer of the church property?

The congregation heard the pastor's deep concern this week. The sermon embraced an emotional issue. Afterward at the door, a few said, "Nice sermon, Pastor," but all went home to live their lives as they had the week before and the week before that. "Is this all there is to my preaching ministry?" asks the pastor.

The soloist who worked hard on the music that had been carefully chosen to augment the pastor's sermon finds herself asking the same question. "Is this all there is? I offered this song to God as an act of worship, and the people clapped when I finished as though it was meant to be a performance for *them*. There must be more to my music ministry."

If this is all there is, why take the time? Some leaders feel they have become engaged in a pointless investment of time and energy. Others are frustrated with performing institutional maintenance rather than engaging in vital ministry and mission. In today's changing society, people are saying, "Grandmom and Granddad had the time, Mom and Dad tried to do it all, and we simply don't need or want one more thing to do."

Why Do People Seek Out the Church?

What are we looking for? Why go to church anyway? There was a time in our society when high value was placed on achieving a certain status in churches and clubs. Churches realized that the sooner a new member was placed on a board or committee, the more quickly that person would become assimilated into the life of the congregation. Appointments were soon followed by elected offices. This method worked for many years. People felt a certain satisfaction in serving on a committee or chairing a board. For the most part, those days are gone.

Many traditional church structures were organized or reorganized during those years. These churches were burdened with more structure than was needed. As a result, some churches have more positions to fill than they have people to fill them. Nominating committees beg people to accept invitations to serve. In one church, a desperate nominating committee member said to a prospective nominee, "Please take this job. You don't have to *do* anything." In more than a few churches, new members are quickly asked to be deacons or members of the governing council. Too often the result is inadequate leadership or an abundance of people doing unnecessary jobs.

On the other hand, we can find churches in which laity are merely members of the audience. They attend, watch the show, and perhaps converse in a small group. That's the extent of their engagement. Lay leadership comes only from a select inner circle.

For vast numbers of laity, both patterns of church life leave something to be desired. More and more people drift away from church or switch from church to church seeking something they can't find. Yet there are those who come, thereby opening themselves to leadership possibilities. What are they looking for?

Fellowship and Community

One of the true strengths of many churches is fellowship. Human beings are attracted to places where they are welcomed as part of a community. These kinds of places make them feel better. Many churches pride themselves in being friendly, when in actuality, they are closed communities. Visitors find themselves standing at the edge of the room during the coffee hour while church members talk happily among themselves. They are oblivious to the guests. Healthy churches are characterized by genuine fellowship. When the local church is a caring community, truly open to outsiders, the church will likely grow.

Good fellowship is enhanced by all the components of positive group dynamics and is a key factor in fostering leader development. In this atmosphere of community and fellowship, however, two critical leadership problems begin to emerge.

1. *Assertion of authority in order to fill ego needs.* Some people seem to want to be in charge of something whether they have the necessary skills or not. If these individuals are allowed to be "in charge," dangers lie along the path. Nearly everyone enjoys a bit of an ego boost when selected to be a leader. But those who are psychologically maladjusted bring a host of challenges to the group they serve. The wise church will surround these people with love, pray for them, and even assist when possible in getting appropriate help for them. These are acts of healing. Leadership will come later.

2. *Perpetual neediness.* The church often does a tremendously good job of ministering to broken people—as it should. Almost all people will encounter a time of brokenness in their lives and

will be ministered to by a caring church. But some people become addicted to the attention of a caring community. They begin to believe the ministry of the church is about them. When these people take perpetual neediness into the leadership arena, trouble will result.

Worship and Inspiration

Many people seek out a church for the weekly worship experiences. Worship today, as practiced in mainline and moderate evangelical churches, is mostly about connecting with friends, hearing the pastor's sermon, being inspired by the musicians, or enjoying the performance of the worship leaders. At its worst, it is boring, wishy-washy, and sleep-inducing. More often, though, it is more or less "adequate." The problem is that "adequate" simply is not magnetic. Worship is at its best when it is authentic. Authenticity in turn engenders magnetism. Visitors sense that leaders and followers are sincerely seeking to be God's people in this place. Authentic worship attracts authentic leaders. ("Offer meaningful worship opportunities" is one of the church's seven steps toward wholeness discussed in chapter 7.)

Music

Some people are attracted to a church by its music—whether the attraction is to the praise team, the old hymns, or the concert organist. In the last half century, music has more often been blamed for tearing churches apart than acclaimed for bringing them together. Music has had to bear the brunt of what have been dubbed "worship wars." Both those on the "traditional" side and those on the "contemporary" side have sometimes been irrational, rigid, and ridiculous in their absolute confidence in the rightness of their cause. It is also important to note that through the years, congregations have been exposed to a great deal of atrocious church music in both traditional and contemporary styles.

No wonder potential leaders are disillusioned. They see the weakness in statements like "We're sorry we can't do any traditional music; we won't get any new members that way." Or "I'm sorry, but we *have* to sing all six verses of the hymn, because that's the way it's written. And we'll sing it slowly so we don't miss anything." Or "Our church sings only contemporary music" when *contemporary* is mentally defined as "songs that were new when I was in college." (One pastor was preparing the order of music for praise time. His teenage son glanced at the computer screen as he walked by. "Oh, Dad, not 'Majesty.' That was written before I was born!" The son obviously had a different perspective on what is "contemporary.")

At its best, music enhances the message of the day, inspires praise, and contributes to a sense of awe as well as a spirit of commitment among the worshippers. Music carefully planned and skillfully led can be a blessing. Being part of a congregation that is open to a wide variety of music styles—not as performance, but as worship—is an even greater blessing.

Learning Opportunities

Some are attracted to a church by a first-rate educational program. However, education in the church suffers from exactly the same problem faced by education in the secular world—it has become a sideline rather than a focus. Too often in the church, the only qualification for teaching is a willingness to do so—the "any warm body will do" syndrome. Many church school teachers haven't been taught how to teach.

Furthermore, just as in the secular world where emphasis has been placed on learning facts that can be regurgitated for standardized tests, in too many churches, this same teaching pattern has emerged. The objective appears to be to indoctrinate children rather than help them become lifelong learners who grow, think, discuss, and ponder in a safe and encouraging environment.

Education remains an important component of the church's ministry, even though it may not be the primary draw it was during the heyday of the Sunday church school. At its best, the teaching arm of the church is creative and stimulating. Bible study informs how we live our lives. Its highest aspiration is the encouragement of wisdom.

An Encounter with God

Many seek out a church to find God. A vital church is a group of people who cultivate a fertile field where others can encounter God. Of course, God may be encountered anywhere. The challenge is to be prepared to recognize God and respond. This preparation can happen in the church through worship, teaching, fellowship, and music. It may then be used in the church and in the world in a host of fruitful experiences.

After 9/11, people turned to churches in droves. Church leaders quickly prepared for a new Great Awakening, but the surge lasted from only a few weeks to a few months. It is possible that many of those post–9/11 seekers didn't find what they were looking for in the church: God. Churches need to help people know how to connect with God in the whole of their lives, and not just in church.

So Who Are the People We Find When We Open the Doors?

Remember the child's finger play: "Here's the church. Here's the steeple. Open the doors, and see all God's people"? We've examined the elements that draw us to a church. Who are the people we find when we get there?

Churches are populated and impacted by regular attendees, lay leaders, clergy, and external faith leaders (the authors, denominational staff, and parachurch leaders who inform the discussion about the church). It helps to understand the way all four groups impact local church life and the recruitment and cultivation of leadership. In the healthy body of Christ, the distinguishing marks of the four groups are somewhat muted. At times the regular attendee becomes a leader and vice versa. External faith leaders also function as local church members and leaders. But what are the unique roles of each?

Regular attendees. These are the people who simply attend a church. In a healthy church, they move from being curious visitors to engaged members. They may from time to time take on leadership responsibilities within the church. The primary way regular attendees impact the life of a particular church body is by demonstrating the results of all the opportunities for preparation the church provides, such as worship, music, and education.

Lay leaders. Lay leaders are those who help a congregation prepare for ministry in the world. Lay leaders help educate and motivate pew sitters to be faith leaders in daily life. Lay leaders serve as deacons, trustees, council members, outreach coordinators, Christian educators, youth leaders, and in numerous other roles. Lay leaders are stewards of the encouragement ministry. They promote joy, hope, and love.

To remember that lay leaders work both inside and outside the church is of vital importance. The "inside" work may be easier to understand than the "outside" work, because the ministries are set forth in official church documents. The "outside" work remains vague.

The outside lay leaders are those who have accepted God's call to be Christ's hands and feet in the world. They do the work of Christ in the world—even more than in the church. A physician in Kansas City shared that his church was upset with him because he didn't spend more time serving on church boards and committees. But from his perspective, he was an arm of the body of Christ serving as an agent of healing. Could his church have experienced transformation if they had realized that the physician was indeed a key leader of the body?

The clergy. Pastors are the church's chief motivators and leader developers. They help congregants make the vital connection between faith on Sunday and faith on Monday. They teach, preach, and love the members and the members' ministries. Pastors guide congregants in understanding the various roles required for fostering spiritual growth and discipleship; they help everyone learn what it means to be part of Christ's body. Moreover, they aid congregants in inspiring others to follow Jesus.

External faith leaders. External faith leaders are most effective at supporting the regular attendees' and leaders' roles. As with lay leaders, external faith leaders' work is both inside and outside the local church. Their "outside" work takes them into the wider arena of encouragement and facilitation with groups of clergy and churches.

They're Here Today but Gone Tomorrow

We've examined the elements that may attract people to a church. Then we briefly showcased the people who make up the church body. Now we ask again, where have all the leaders gone? Quality lay leadership is vanishing, and a primary reason is disengagement. The most frequent cause of disengagement is disillusionment. Members, lay leaders, clergy, and external leaders alike ask, "Is this all there is?" Understanding the vague dissatisfaction that weighs on leaders is essential if that dissatisfaction is to be overcome and leaders are to be encouraged, developed, and valued. Indeed, it is critical if current and new leaders are to be productive.

Three subtle elements contribute to disillusionment and the resulting act of disengagement: purpose and structure, individual resistance, and misuse of leaders.

Purpose and Structure

Consider the congregation that believed a church was required to have twelve deacons because there were twelve disciples. We get in trouble when we mimic the wrong things. The number wasn't magic. And obviously, one of those placed on Jesus' team was not a team player. The church based a structural decision on the wrong detail of Jesus' ministry and leadership style. (We'll look at Jesus' leadership style in more detail in chapter 2.) Instead of imitating the number of disciples Jesus chose, the church should have selected the number of deacons necessary to effectively carry out the deacon ministry in that particular church.

We can take a lesson about purpose and structure from the Union Pacific Railroad. On the outside, the Union Pacific's new

---

VISION: BUILDING AMERICA

Our vision symbolizes the Union Pacific experience for all the people whose lives we touch. It connects the importance of UP's rail transportation to America's economy, honors the generations that preceded us and is the promise for the generations that will follow us.

Mission: The Men and Women of Union Pacific Are Dedicated to Serve.

Union Pacific works for the good of our customers, our shareholders and one another. Our commitment defines us and drives the economic strength of our company and our country.

Values: *Focus on Performance.* Our concentration and determination will drive our safety, customer satisfaction and quality results.

Ensure High Ethical Standards. Our reputation will always be a source of pride for our employees and a bond with our customers, shareholders and community partners.

Work as a Team. We are all part of the same team, and working together to reach our common goals is one of our strengths. Communication and respect are the foundation of great teamwork.

---

headquarters building in Omaha, Nebraska looks just like any other office building. Yet if you look carefully behind the glass walls on the second floor at any time of the day you happen to pass by, you'll see dozens of people on treadmills and other exercise machines. The vision and purpose of the organization influenced the unique qualities of this particular building's structure. The "Company Overview" of Union Pacific's website (www.up.com) is highly instructive. Take a look at the company's vision and mission statement on page 11.[1]

Did you notice that Union Pacific's vision and mission is all about people? If you were to visit their website, you'd find their information about the actual railroad appears *after* their crystal clear focus on people. Their marketing priority suggests they are neither in the business of running railroads nor making money by operating railroads. Instead, their business is people seeking to serve (serving the economy, serving the heritage and the future, serving the country) by running railroads. If the "men and women of the Union Pacific are dedicated to serve," the company must see to it that they are given the opportunity to be healthy. The company's mission statement explains the busy exercise facility on the second floor. People are this railroad's most important resource.

Compare Union Pacific's mentality with that of an unnamed nonprofit educational organization we visited. They proudly stated their mission but then quickly went on to declare that their business was raising money. How much more effective it would have been if they had stated, "Our business is to provide donors and foundations with the satisfaction of investing in the development of high-quality leaders, thereby stimulating more giving from existing donors and new giving from others."

The clearer the relationship between purpose and structure, the more attractive will be the leadership opportunities. The structure, whether the physical building or the organizational framework, must be compatible with the purpose of the church, or a leadership vacuum will eventually evolve. The vacuum occurs because most people won't willingly remain in a state of tension. If the demands on leadership don't make sense in light of the mission of the church, most leaders will break under the tension. Others will simply drift away, while still others will perform poorly.

Individual Resistance

Churches have also lost leaders because members encounter resistance in their daily lives. Trying to speak for or defend the church is a tall order. Some church leaders have given up trying. There are two basic types of resistance to the church: passive and active.

1. *Passive resistance.* Some people have simply never been in a church and have no idea why it would have any appeal for them. They are not particularly negative about the church; they just don't think much about it. In this category are some of those we call the "unchurched." Also included are people who have simply drifted away from church life.

2. *Active resistance.* Active resistors are people who don't like the church. Some of the "unchurched" fit in this category if they have never been involved in a church but have learned from friends, family, or the media that churches are bad. They may talk about the hypocrisy of the church while never having been directly exposed to a local church body. Other active resistors are the "dechurched," people who have left a church out of anger, violation of trust, frustration, or personal hurt. Many dechurched individuals have developed a strong strain of resistance to the church.

How many people do you know who fit either of these categories? Jan used to be a member of your church, but now she's among the dechurched. She's adrift, with no church home, and she's not looking for one either. She once served on the board of trustees and at another time was the Sunday church school superintendent. Obviously, she has leadership skills, but she's been through the leadership mill. The chances of her offering to serve again in any leadership role in a church are nil.

Rex is a good neighbor. He'd do anything to help you out. He's compassionate and often calls just to see how you're doing. He's a spiritual person who connects with God in his own ways, but he's not a churchgoer. He doesn't feel the need to be part of a group on Sunday mornings. He has all the interpersonal challenges he can deal with during the workweek. On weekends he spends time at home enjoying the peace and quiet.

Dale and Mary, along with their young children, Jordan and Allison, were out on the bike trail at 9:30 a.m. last Sunday as you passed by on your way to church. It crossed your mind that it would be good to have several families like them in your church. Dale and Mary, however, reserve Sunday mornings for family time. Many young American families like them consider it a noble thing to do. They're not *against* going to church; instead, they're *in favor* of growing closer as a family. The busy work and school week separates the family into individual routines. Sunday provides them with bonding time.

All three examples reveal laity who could be leaders. Certainly the local body of believers would be richer if they were a part of it. For Jan, Rex, Dale, and Mary, however, the force of either passive or active resistance is more powerful than the attraction of the local church.

Misuse of Leaders

Some leadership patterns in the church damage faith development rather than enhance it. Leaders are often misused.

Leaders are overworked. Sometimes we expect too much from our leaders. We've followed the old adage "If you want something done, ask a busy person." Still, reality limits us to a finite number of hours in a day. Leaders who are overworked will continue trying to "do it all" for a while, but burnout lurks on the horizon. When it hits, the results are lamentable. Leaders and followers alike suffer.

Leaders are given jobs and titles that inflate their egos. This manner of misuse is very subtle. For a person to work up through the leadership ranks of a church or any institution seems to be a natural process. In many cases, this progression works well. Fred served as a committee member for two terms before he was chosen as the chairperson. By the time he became the chair, he had learned the ropes and proved to be an effective group leader. On the other hand, Judy, who was elected to a committee in a sister church, wanted to be the chair from the day she said yes to the nominating committee. She knew she could do a good job, and besides, she had a lot of ideas about the way things should be done. She voiced her opinions and offered helpful suggestions. When she found herself in the chairperson's slot at the beginning of her second year, she was aglow. She also forgot what it was like to be a team player and listen to others. She was the chair, and the committee would operate as she saw fit.

Leaders are pigeonholed. In rounding out the annual slate of church officers, the nominating committee may try to match secular jobs with church jobs. For example, the banker is asked to serve on the board of trustees or finance committee. And why not? She knows a lot about money. The truth is, the banker works with financial figures every day all week long. What she is really interested in when she comes to church is helping guide the lives of the junior high students with whom she easily relates. Who knew? Who asked?

Leaders may be square pegs in round holes. This leader development deterrent is closely related to pigeonholing. If our banker in the previous example had succumbed to pigeonholing, she could have become a square peg in a round hole. Drew, a junior high teacher in the public schools, found himself in that very predicament. Soon after he joined the church, he was invited to teach a young adult Sunday church school class. The superintendent thought Drew would enjoy the change from teaching junior high students to teaching his peers. Eager to serve wherever needed, Drew quickly said yes. While he taught the class faithfully week after week, he found the numbers on the attendance records to be dwindling. People had stopped attending the class because Drew taught the class the way he knew how to teach, using the approaches that worked in the junior high classroom. He was, indeed, a square peg in a round hole. As Pastor Anne got to know Drew better, she discovered his passion for spiritual development. When Drew was later elected to the diaconate, the ministry was a good fit.

Leaders feel they fail the fitness test. Introspection is not a bad thing. The examination of oneself can lead to improved production. When asked to serve in a spiritual leadership role, we rightfully ask, "Am I holy enough?" When asked to complete a task, we query, "Can't someone else do this better than I can?" When entering a new leadership role, we wonder, "What will they think of me? The church sees me differently than I see myself." The problem with all of these introspective issues is that they point at other human beings.

Against whose standards shall we attempt to measure ourselves? Holiness is a God-related issue. Likewise, we measure our performance against the best that God calls us to do. Finally, we do best to focus on living a life pleasing to God rather than stressing our minds with what others think of us. In other words, *God* administers the fitness test. Taking the self-administered fitness test using human standards deters leadership development.

A disillusioned leader needs a lot of faith and trust to change course and move from the disengagement mode back into a fulfilled ministry role. For some, it never happens. For others, time helps the psyche to heal. If the church has found the prescription for health and a new or renewed missional focus, disengaged leaders may reengage.

The Church as the Body of Christ

The healthy church constantly seeks to be the body of Christ—whether it takes the form of a neighborhood church, a rural church, a megachurch, a traditional church, or a contemporary church. Size of a congregation and location have nothing to do with whether a church is functioning as the body of Christ. Leadership with a keen understanding of purpose has everything to do with it.

What if church leaders, instead of desperately chasing after popular church models in a misdirected attempt to salvage an institution or a salary, refocused on what it means to actually be the body of Christ regardless of the consequences? We might find a church in which all people are valued, the focus is outward rather than inward, continual refocusing occurs to keep the main thing the main thing, and the body is characterized by vision, love, action, and joy. That's the challenging goal.

How can the church create an environment in which leaders and followers can actually *be* the church—the body of Christ? How can members *be* the church rather than just *go* to church? As believers, we are part of a community formed by God—the body of Christ. "Christ is like a single body, which has many parts; it is still one body, even though it is made up of different parts" (1 Corinthians 12:12, TEV). In Ephesians we read, "So when each separate part works as it should, the whole body grows and builds itself up through love" (4:16, TEV). Our church is not just a place to drop in on Sunday for a "Jesus fix." Rather, it is a group of people who have the potential to be a nurturing; joy-permeated; profoundly loving, passionate, vital group of people with whom we choose to walk in life and do the ministry to which God has called us. To overcome "Is that all there is?" thinking in the church, the church must renew its understanding of what it means to be the body of Christ.

According to noted clergyman and author Ray Stedman, "The church is a living organism. In the physical body, the hand moves when the brain says to. So too the members of Jesus' spiritual body take direction from Him as our Head. Jesus gives each member gifts and talents, making himself alive within his church. He equips his people to love one another and to serve in unity in his kingdom."[2] A popular movement is underway among some free churches to demand a stronger hierarchy in the church body. However, a stronger hierarchy is not what is needed. What is needed are humble leaders and followers who seek together to discern the leading of the Spirit. Jesus is the head, the cornerstone. "Christ himself gave the apostles, the prophets, the evangelists, the pastors and teachers, to equip his people for works of service, so that the body of Christ may be built up until we all reach unity in the faith and in the knowledge of the Son of God and become mature, attaining to the whole measure of the fullness of Christ" (Ephesians 4:11-13, NIV).

The church is the body of Christ—a living organism. Body life is sustained by the very Source of life. As we rely on that divine eternal Source, we never have to ask, "Is this all there is?" Instead, we are propelled into kingdom-building action. Our day-to-day activities become acts of worship. Freed, motivated, and empowered, we become the hands and feet of Christ in a hurting and confused world.

QUESTIONS for Personal Reflection or Group Discussion

1. Compare and contrast Union Pacific's mission statement with your church's mission statement. What similarities and differences can you identify?

2. Did your church's mission statement grow out of the DNA of your church, or was it superimposed by a group of people who believed having a mission statement would be a catalyst for being the body of Christ? If it has not emerged from your church's DNA, what must happen to make it transformational rather than a sharp slogan to memorize?

3. In what ways does the existing statement guide your church's planning process?

4. How does your church's mission statement foster leadership development? In what other ways are individuals cultivated for future leadership within your congregation?

5. How do you participate in fulfilling your church's mission statement?

6. Do you sense that you are part of your church—the body of Christ, or do you just go to church? Why do you feel as you do?

7. What helps a newcomer to your church feel comfortable, appreciated, and respected rather than overwhelmed, invisible, or cornered?

8. How can churches offer more opportunities for individuals to engage in the kind of leadership experiences that will feed their souls and energize their action without consuming them?

Notes

1. Union Pacific Railroad, "Company Overview: Company Vision/Mission Statement," http://www.up.com/aboutup/corpo rate_info/uprrover.shtml (accessed January 19, 2012).

2. Ray Stedman, "Body Life." http://www.raystedman.org/the matic-studies/body-life (accessed June 21, 2010).

CHAPTER 2

Where Did Jesus Learn to Lead?

Lessons from a Master Carpenter
An "As It Might Have Been" Story

It was nearly dusk. Jesus paused before leaving the shop and looked back. He knew the private years of his life were over. Tomorrow he would head out. He knew what was to come would be public, but the past was his to treasure. He chuckled when he remembered the only really public part of his growing-up years—the amazing visit to the temple when he was twelve. A couple of the older women still teased him about the stir he caused. He had never again seen his parents so distraught. But other than that, his life had been his own. This simple, quiet life of a boy growing into manhood had been a gift. He would always be grateful.

He was going to miss the shop. His dad had been a carpenter, and he and one of his brothers had become carpenters too. His dad had always made the work interesting. Jesus had been in charge after his dad died. He knew his brother would carry on the tradition of quality work for a fair price. He allowed himself just a few moments to think of what it might be like if he stayed. Nevertheless, he was clear in his understanding that it was time to begin his life's intended work. Besides, his brother had a right to get out from under Joseph's and Jesus' shadows and become a noted carpenter in his own right.

Their dad had been amazing. Everyone said, "Joseph the carpenter gives you even more than you ask." That's why everyone trusted him. They knew the product would display quality workmanship.

Jesus recalled an incident when he was about fourteen years old. That summer he had helped Joseph craft a yoke for their neighbor, Micah. Micah was never happy. As a rule, he was mean-spirited and a chronic complainer. From Jesus' teenage perspective, he wasn't sure they needed to be quite as precise on this particular yoke. He asked his dad, "Why does this yoke have to be so perfect? It's very good as it is. Why keep working it? It's only for Micah."

"But son," Joseph replied, "that's exactly the reason. It's for Micah. Let's give him a wonderful gift— whether he realizes it or not."

They worked until it was a truly fine yoke. When Micah came to pick it up, he was in a bad mood, as usual. He harrumphed and grumped, paid his bill, and went on his way.

Joseph shook his head and murmured, "Poor Micah."

Jesus asked, "What do you mean?"

Joseph smiled and answered, "I'm afraid we may have frustrated him. He is not going to be able to find anything wrong with that yoke. But maybe one day, while putting it on his oxen, he will have to concede that it is a good thing to know a good carpenter."

Jesus smiled, remembering that day and so many

others like it. Joseph had lived a life that reflected the core of who he was. Joseph didn't have to stand up in the synagogue and give a speech. Who and what he was became evident in all he did. Jesus knew God had used his earthly parents to help prepare him for his public life.

As he thanked God again for his family, he was filled with admiration for the way his dad and mom had guided him, loved him, and served as examples for him to follow. Oh, it was a traditional home, to be sure. Joseph earned the money, and Mary cared for the house and cooked the food. Yet, Jesus knew, there was something in their relationship that was different from the relationships of many other couples. Although their family had the normal joys and sorrows of any family, it was always clear that his parents not only loved each other but also respected each other.

Through the years, Jesus thought about them often. They were male and female, each having been created in the image of God. Each was unique and gifted, recognizing the individuality of the other and of each of their children.

Jesus slowly looked around one last time before he turned and left the shop. He knew his mother had prepared his favorite meal for this, his last night at home.

Learning Leadership from Jesus

We can imagine how growing up in Mary and Joseph's home and working in the carpentry shop helped Jesus form his perspectives and understanding of the world. While it is impossible to fully understand Jesus' identity as both human and divine, it is easy to accept that the home in which Jesus grew up had a formative impact on his earthly ministry. If one can accept the God of the universe coming to earth as a baby born in a stable, it follows that the baby was meant to have the very human experience of growing up from infancy through childhood and adolescence to adulthood.

Jesus must have learned a great deal from his parents. Because of them, he saw and understood life through human eyes. But his wisdom came from God.

Many years ago in a news feature on a Philadelphia television station, a reporter interviewed an eye surgeon. This particular doctor was recognized for his tremendous surgical skill. The reporter asked the doctor what made him so gifted. The doctor responded that anyone could learn to do eye surgery. The reporter pressed back, asking the doctor again what made him so extraordinary. The doctor then quietly replied that it takes wisdom, and wisdom is God-given. Then, after a thoughtful pause, he offered significant biblical insight into how one receives divine wisdom. Echoing James 1:5, he said that God gives wisdom, but we have to ask for it.

Jesus had earthly knowledge and skills, and he had divine wisdom. Once his ministry began, he invited people to join him in his ministry. He got more out of people than they could have expected of themselves. We can't equal Jesus, but we can learn from him how to be better laypeople in our workplaces as well as better leaders and teachers of leaders in our churches.

A common illustration of Jesus' leadership style is that of a shepherd. Shepherd and sheep language is common throughout the Bible, and rightfully so. The Judean hillsides were populated by shepherds and sheep. Christians are especially familiar with Jesus' metaphor, "I am the good shepherd" (John 10:11, 14, NRSV). Every metaphor has its possibilities and limitations, and this metaphor can be interpreted in at least two ways.

First, some people today desperately want the metaphor of shepherd to justify an authoritarian system of governance in the church. They see the shepherd as all-knowing. The sheep, which cannot or will not think for themselves, only succeed as they mindlessly follow the shepherd. When this leadership perspective is promoted, the pastor assumes a godlike role in the congregation. This is not a healthy model.

The second, and we believe stronger, interpretation of the shepherd metaphor is that of a leader who deeply understands the flock. Whereas leadership and lordship are not synonymous, leadership and servanthood are. Jesus told his disciples, "You know that among the Gentiles those whom they recognize as their rulers lord it over them, and their great ones are tyrants over them. But it is not so among you; but whoever wishes to become great among you must be your servant" (Mark 10:42-43, NRSV). The good shepherd leads with patient love and compassion. This rendering suggests humility, assurance, good communication skills, and the intent to help each person reach his or her potential.

Leading with Humility

The word *humility* is not popular in our culture. We often equate the characteristic with weakness. In our mind's eye, we see a humble person as limp, drab, lacking power and punch. These are false understandings. Humility signals extraordinary strength of character.

■ *Humility fosters openness.* Humble leaders recognize their own strengths and weaknesses and operate accordingly.
■ *Humility nurtures generosity.* Humble leaders place the spotlight on the persons whom they are leading rather than on themselves.
■ *Humility demands accountability.* Humble leaders do the right thing because it is the right thing.
■ *Humility builds trust.* Humble leaders admit their mistakes.
■ *Humility inspires followers.* Humble leaders connect with the people they lead.

Jesus exhibited humility. He closed a discourse on servanthood by explaining to his disciples, "The Son of Man came not to be served but to serve, and to give his life a ransom for many" (Mark 10:45, NRSV). During his final Passover celebration, he clearly led by example when he washed his disciples' feet (John 13:1-17).

While Jesus knew that his life on earth would soon end in public humiliation on the cross, he also knew it would not be long before he once again took his place on the throne with God in heaven. During this festival time, Jesus might have chosen to focus on the imminent glory that would be his to enjoy. Instead, he rose from the table and put aside his robe, just as he put aside his position. Then he wrapped a towel around his waist, poured water into a basin, and washed his disciples' feet. The Lord of all performed a task customarily given to the lowliest servants in his day. In stooping down, he humbly poured out his love in service to others.

Chet was the first layperson to serve as a regional executive minister in one particular US mainline denomination. He left his role as a top corporate executive to serve about fifty churches in the Midwest. In addition to helping this organization of churches focus on their servant ministries, his denominational work included providing pastoral care for clergy and placement assistance for both clergy and congregations. He carried out these tasks with utmost humility. As one would expect from a humble leader, he never boasted. He shied away from public adulation. He always took time for the people who crossed his path. He listened to what they had to say, expressed interest in them as well as their families, and articulated his care and concern in memorable ways. His compelling modesty endeared him to people of all ages. The board that hired Chet had tapped the very root of the church populous—the laity. They had recognized his call to denominational work and wisely stepped aside to watch God work through this remarkable servant leader.

Leading with Assurance

Humility is only effective in leaders who understand themselves. To be sure, a leader is most effective when confident, but the leader dares not let this confidence mutate into arrogance. Rather, an effective leader is self-assured. At its best, this calm sense of self allows the leader to do what must be done. Humility and assurance balance each other.

Recall the metaphor of Jesus as shepherd. Place this image of compassion alongside the life image of Jesus as a trained carpenter. The carpenter knows how to work with resources and tools to deliver a desired outcome. The carpenter envisions the completed project and plans accordingly. The carpenter has the assurance that the task at hand can be skillfully completed and will be appreciated by its user. Both of these images—shepherd and carpenter—inform our understanding of Jesus' leadership style.

In Matthew 7:28-29 the people are described as being amazed by the way Jesus taught with authority. He had confidence that sprang from the spiritual assurance of God's wisdom within him and the practical assurance of knowing how to do the task.

But what happened the day Jesus upended the money changers' tables in the temple? (The incident is recorded in all four Gospels: Matthew 21:12-17; Mark 11:15-19; Luke 19:45-48; and John 2:13-17). On that day, humility did not look like shy, retiring cooperation. Jesus was confronted with a situation of enormous greed. In the face of gross injustice, he acted. The system of extorting money from the pilgrims who came to the temple probably began as a fairly simple system to provide pilgrims with animals they needed for sacrifice. Through the years, the system had grown into a corrupt, exploitative travesty.

Jesus' demeanor when he cleansed the temple was not consistent with the way we generally have known him to operate. Confronted with grave injustice against the poor, Jesus rose to an extraordinary situation with a style suited only to such an extreme case.

To understand how a person who demonstrates true humility can have an outburst such as this, it is critical to note that Jesus' act was not self-aggrandizing. If a person has a public outburst, even to defend the poor, with a sense of how well it will play in the press, he or she will display no humility (or even honesty). Jesus' act was in direct response to the situation. Whether he was acclaimed or condemned did not matter to him.

The difference between Jesus and us is that he had a level of assurance and confidence to which we can only aspire. Are our acts of righteous indignation motivated by the love of God or by our own needs, wants, or desires?

Leading by Practicing Good Communication Skills

Good conversation has three parts: speaking, listening, and silence. Most of us focus on speaking. If this were a horse race, "speaking" would come across the finish line about thirty lengths ahead of number two—"listening." Have you ever seen a horse race with as wide a gap as that? Second place goes to "listening." Most of us do it poorly. Third place goes to the spaces...the silence...the time for mulling over...for thinking. The temptation in conversation is to fill all the gaps. In our horse race, "silence" would barely be out of the gate as "speaking" finished the race. All three of these aspects—speaking, listening, and silence—must be practiced in order for the mature fruit of communication to develop. That desired fruit is understanding.

To become better listeners, we must avoid some common behaviors. The *Communication Briefings* newsletter lists some of the hindrances to good listening:

■ *Mind reading.* If we're trying to determine what the speaker is *really* thinking or feeling, we hear little or nothing.
■ *Rehearsing.* Mentally preparing our next response causes us to tune out the speaker.
■ *Filtering.* Filtering or hearing only what we want to hear is also known as selective listening.
■ *Daydreaming.* If we think about something other than what the

speaker is saying, we may have to ask them to repeat themselves.

■ *Identifying*. When we try to relate everything we hear to our own experiences, it is likely that we aren't hearing what is being said.

■ *Comparing*. By comparing ourselves to the messenger, we focus on ourselves rather than the message.

■ *Derailing*. We derail a conversation when we change the subject too soon and, as a result, signal our disinterest in anything the speaker has to say.

■ *Sparring*. By belittling or discounting what is being said, we also signal our disinterest.

■ *Placating*. Agreeing with everything the speaker says simply to be nice or to avoid conflict doesn't signal good listening skills.[1]

The cross-cultural story of Jesus and the woman of Samaria (John 4) reveals Jesus' ability to search and understand the human heart and establishes him as a master communicator. En route from Judea to Galilee, Jesus chose to pass through Samaria. Jews generally avoided the region altogether, for they viewed Samaritans with disdain. Jesus' unconventional choice took him to the city of Sychar. Tired from his journey, Jesus sat down by the well. The Bible tells us it was about noon.

While he rested, Jesus initiated a conversation with a Samaritan woman who came to the well to fill her water container. His simple request for a drink of water immediately put her on guard, for no Jewish rabbi would speak to a woman in public. Yet Jesus engaged her in memorable dialogue that interwove the literal with the metaphorical. After moving back and forth from the mention of everyday drinking water to spiritual life-giving water, they progressed to the subject of her marital status. Jesus exposed her situation, not to condemn her, but rather to help her understand that she needed the living water he offered. She quickly recognized that what he said was true. Somewhat embarrassed, she changed the subject from the personal to the theological—a religious debate about the proper place to worship. Jesus skillfully seized the opportunity to expand her understanding and increase her faith. In the end, this conversation inspired her to tell others about her afternoon at the well. As a result, many people in Sychar came to believe in Jesus.

Two thirsty people came to the well. Jesus saw an opportunity based on their common need. In his self-assured manner, he engaged the Samaritan woman in a life-changing conversation. In Jesus' exchange with her, as in his discussions with many others along the way, his most profound teaching was embedded in ordinary conversation. Today leaders and followers confront situations more effectively with good communication skills practiced with ease. Everyone is better off when they take the time and energy for conversation.

Lee Hamilton, a former congressperson and president of the Woodrow Wilson International Center, was interviewed on National Public Radio in 2010 near the time of his retirement from more than forty years of public service. Having served in Congress during the Cold War, he had opportunities to meet with Soviet parliamentarians. He described settings where both he and the Soviets read speeches. The speeches were commonly followed by toasts to one another, to world peace, and to prosperous lives for their descendants. But nothing happened. This went on year after year until they changed the protocol. They discontinued the speech-making process, and instead, they began talking with one another. He cited that change as the beginning of the end of the Cold War.[2] As we practice good communication skills and seek to understand each other, situations begin to change.

Leading by Focusing on Potential

Elementary school teachers learn early in their careers that a solution to dealing with a troublemaker is to assign the child a position of responsibility. Children who are recognized for their potential and who are moving purposefully toward it are more likely to be satisfied and less contentious. The same is true with many adults. This principle can be used in the church.

Jesus saw potential in some surprising people. The story of Zacchaeus certainly caught our attention as children in Sunday church school. As a tax collector who skimmed off some of the collection for himself, Zacchaeus was not respected or liked. The children's song describes him as a "wee little man." Zacchaeus wanted to see Jesus, so he climbed up in a tree to get above the crowd. Jesus spotted him, asked him to come down, and announced that he would be staying at Zacchaeus's house. Jesus saw beyond Zacchaeus's occupation, stature, and even his flawed character.

The story of Zacchaeus is a powerful one for us. We are taught from an early age, "Don't judge a book by its cover." And yet we do that very thing over and over. We are guilty of judgment based on surface observation.

Years ago, during the congressional Watergate hearings, many of us were glued to the television, watching history in the making. A sidelight to the whole scandal was the number of people who talked about how they wished Representative Barbara Jordan would become president. The majority of people who made this observation never would have paid that much attention to Jordan if they hadn't been so engaged in watching the outcome of the hearings. In the course of watching, they became deeply impressed with someone they never would have considered as presidential material. Instead of seeing someone who was female, older, and African American, they began to see an astute congressperson who was well educated, well prepared, and wise. Health issues prevented Jordan from continuing her political career, but many who watched her on television realized she was a true leader.

The process of identifying potential leaders requires getting to know people better. Walt was the pastor of a church in North

Dakota. Each year prior to Easter, Walt assembled all the people who had joined the church in the preceding year. He explained that he needed them to work on a craft project. He acknowledged that this task was probably far below their expertise but that he really needed their help. The winsome magnetism of his personality convinced them. The process seemed preposterous, and yet it worked year after year.

The group gathered and found out they were going to make butterflies! These butterflies were constructed of many colors of tissue paper glued over wire frames. College professors, construction workers, car salespersons, military officers, moms, dads, and kids sat together, worked together, and got to know one another. On Easter Sunday morning, the congregation arrived to find the anticipated joy. Above their heads, the butterflies were flying. The "volunteer" crew had hung their creations from the ceiling with clear fishing line. The "skies" of the sanctuary were full of butterflies that flew from Easter to Pentecost.

What does a butterfly craft project have to do with developing leaders? In the process of this simple creative process, the new members became better acquainted with one another and with their pastor. They probably agreed to the project because it was of very limited duration and because of the pastor's persuasiveness. But the result was "ownership" of a church project. Longer term members sought out the new members to compliment them on their creative work and to tell stories of their own experience of working on butterflies in previous years. Leaders began to emerge from the new group.

Each year someone would say, "We should just use the butterflies from last year." But when someone went to get them, there were never enough. Some had been "lost" and a batch of new ones had to be made. The annual project enhanced the congregation's worship experience and expanded the leadership pool. Churches are continually gifted with potential leadership, but that leadership must be identified, cultivated, and provided with viable opportunities. The process takes time.

Jesus' selection of his disciples is probably the most convincing example of the way his leadership style focused on potential. If any of us had been consultants to Jesus on the selection of members of his leadership team, would we have recommended the Twelve? Primary among them were men in the seafood business. Add to the personnel list a tax collector and an additional contingent of obscure individuals, and we have Jesus' ministry team—a group that changed the world.

A closer look reveals a ragtag crew. Over the course of a year, Jesus observed these ordinary people with their common, yet unique, tendencies. Time and time again, he watched Simon Peter respond impulsively. He recognized James's and John's volatile temperaments. Thomas proved to be cautious and prone to doubting. Philip, on the other hand, was curious and full of questions. Other Jews labeled Matthew as a traitor and Simon the Zealot as a hard-core nationalist. Yet Jesus chose these along with the traitorous Judas Iscariot and others to form his ministry team.

Temperamental and impulsive, they represented a curious cross-section of the society of their day. They held no prominent positions, nor were they descendants of famous or wealthy individuals. To top it off, no team member had any formal training for this assignment. But each one had potential for this new work. Just like the butterfly crafters, they had the capacity to learn; they were teachable.

Following Empowers Leaders

Good leaders not only know how to lead; they also know how to follow. Jesus perfected both roles. He was a devout follower of God; the human was subject to the divine. Under the power of God's leadership in and through him, Jesus was able to lead others. His disciples in turn began as followers, went out as leaders, came back as followers, and moved out again as leaders. Later in this book we suggest that a leadership model in the church that intentionally taps this ability to shift from following to leading and back to following is a healthy model for churches. ("The Simple Circle" found on pages 125–128, is one way to achieve this desired rotation.)

To follow a leader requires that we respect him or her. As followers, we also desire respect from our leaders. Not to be confused with tolerance, respect suggests high regard and a close relationship. Toward the end of his Good Shepherd discourse, Jesus said, "The Father and I are one" (John 10:30, NRSV). He wanted his listeners to understand that his work and God's work are indistinguishable. Father and Son are completely united in what they do. During his earthly ministry, Jesus responded to spiritual nudgings. He regularly separated himself from his followers to spend time in prayer. Just as Jesus spent time with his earthly father, he also spent time with his heavenly Father learning to lead.

QUESTIONS for Personal Reflection or Group Discussion

1. What is your "as it might have been" image of Jesus in his early years before he entered public ministry?
2. Recall someone who helped you fulfill your potential. How did he or she do it?
3. Is humility a gift or is it learned? What are your reasons for thinking as you do?
4. Assurance and arrogance are close cousins. What makes a person seem self-assured? What makes a person appear arrogant?
5. Which of the three elements—speaking, listening, and remaining silent in order to gain understanding—do you need to cultivate in order to improve your communication skills?
6. What other leadership skills do you believe Jesus exhibited?

Notes

1. "Why We Don't Hear Others," in *The Writing Lab* (West Lafayette, IN: Purdue University Department of English), quoted by Jack Gillespie, ed., *Communication Briefings* 17, no. 2, 1.

2. "Lee Hamilton Shares Memories from His Public Life" (National Public Radio, morning ed., September 27, 2010), http://www.npr.org/templates/story/story.php?storyId=130149474 (accessed September 27, 2010).

CHAPTER 3

Amazing Ingredients for Action

Wouldn't it be great if churches could select leaders simply by identifying the people who are most like Jesus? A checklist of Jesus' leadership characteristics would help nominating committees prepare their annual slate.

There are two problems with this approach to identifying leaders. First, none of us is "enough" like Jesus. Some of us emulate certain characteristics that Jesus displayed, while others of us display an entirely different set of Christlike characteristics. Waiting to find a deacon or a teacher who is like Jesus could slow the nominating process down beyond reason! Second, we need leaders who are genuine. The challenge is that often the personality we display at church is not who we really are. Great leaders are those who are working on personal wholeness. We'll take a look at that process in chapter 6.

That said, there is still something very compelling about finding those who seek to be like Jesus. With all our human flaws, we are still called to walk in his steps. Years ago, Roger Fredrikson wrote a book titled *God Loves the Dandelions*, in which he argued that the church is not a place for hothouse orchids. The church is full of weeds—just regular folks. We gather as dandelions and just do what needs to be done as well as we can. It does not make sense to wait for the orchids to show up and do everything perfectly.[1]

When God builds a church, all the necessary ingredients exist among the people. Congregants or dandelions—whichever term you prefer—are gifted people. The apostle Paul suggested that while God does not gift every leader with identical leadership strengths, God gives *something* to everyone. In Romans 12:6 Paul wrote that "we have gifts that differ according to the grace given to us" (NRSV). And Peter urged his readers to "serve one another with whatever gift each of you has received" (1 Peter 4:10, NRSV).

Local churches utilizing a process of gift discovery and mobilization intentionally focus on leadership strengths. According to Gallup researchers,

> The most effective leaders are always investing in strengths. In the workplace, when an organization's leadership fails to focus on individuals' strengths, the odds of an employee being engaged are a dismal 1 in 11 (9 percent). But when an organization's leadership focuses on the strengths of its employees, the odds soar to almost 3 in 4 (73 percent). When leaders focus on and invest in their employees' strengths, the odds of each person being engaged goes up *eightfold.*[2]

If investing in strengths brings an eightfold return in the workplace, why not apply the same principle in the church? Spiritual gifts are named in Romans 12:6-8; 1 Corinthians 12:7-11, 27-31; and Ephesians 4:7, 11-13. Numerous studies on the subject of spiritual gifts as well as spiritual gift inventory tools are available for purchase. Invest now if you haven't already done so.

People who exercise their spiritual gifts produce fruit. In Galatians 5:22-23, Paul listed the fruit of the Spirit as "love, joy, peace, patience, kindness, generosity, faithfulness, gentleness, and self-control" (NRSV). As with others of Paul's lists recorded in the Bible, this catalogue is probably illustrative rather than exhaustive.

After all, the expressions of the Holy Spirit through our individual personalities defy description.

It is easy to view these expressions as a kind of "nicey nice" or wimpy list of "do-gooder" habits. In reality, the fruit of the Spirit are active, strong, gutsy, powerful, outward-directed actions that involve others. They are outward expressions of Christ within us. In John 15, Jesus described himself as the Vine in whom we, the branches, abide. He said it is our job to bear fruit.

The New English Bible highlights the sometimes-overlooked distinction between spiritual gifts and spiritual fruits. "The harvest of the Spirit is love, joy, peace…" (Galatians 5:22, NEB). The word "harvest" reflects an organic process. We are gifted people who are called to abide in Christ. In turn, producing fruit for the harvest becomes a high priority.

● ● ● ● ● ● ● ● ● ● ● ● ● ● ● ● ●

SUSAN'S STORY

When I was in sixth grade, we studied electricity. My dad took a half day off from work and came to my class to give us a demonstration of how electricity works. He made a model with a battery almost the size of a Pringles potato chip can. The wires went from the battery to a switch and from there to a lightbulb. He showed us how it worked. It was great. We learned, very clearly, that you need a power source if you want something to happen. The demonstration my father presented to the class that day would now look like something out of a history museum. But the learning point is still valid: you have to have a power source.

Our bodies derive power from the food we eat. Even our minds are fed by food. Many in the scientific community would argue that the kind and quality of food we eat has a great deal to do with how well we think. But what about our spirits? As believers, we can tap into an extraordinary source of power—God. What is particularly amazing to me is that we, not God, control the switch. God has given us free will, and God lets us make decisions. God invites us to open the switch and allow divine power to get to us through the various "wires" that are available to us. These wires are "bundled" much like communication cables are. I like to think of the collection of wires as being the spiritual disciplines we practice.

When we use our spiritual gifts, we open the circuit for God's power to flow into us. As we remain connected to the Power Source, we produce fruits such as love, joy, peace, patience, kindness, generosity, faithfulness, gentleness, and self-control.

● ● ● ● ● ● ● ● ● ● ● ● ● ● ● ●

Identifying Leaders

Great church leaders are spiritually mature, or at least are well on the road toward that maturity. Spiritual maturity is not synonymous with long tenure in the congregation. Rather, spiritual maturity involves the use of spiritual gifts in a fruitful manner.

Following are some practical ways to identify leaders. To help in the process, we have included some benefits as well as cautions and suggestions in each category. These categories are not necessarily exclusive of each other. You may even find someone who exhibits the positive qualities of all of these!

1. The Natural Leader

Cynthia is a person who seems to have all the gifts for leadership. Within a fairly short time after joining the church, she begins to become involved in a number of activities. When she serves on a committee or task group, people turn to her for ideas. She and the people are comfortable with her in a leadership role.

Positives: This type of person doesn't need to be trained in how to lead a group, although she will benefit from workshops that refine her leadership skills.

Cautions: Is she capable of following when she is not the leader? Does she overcommit? Over-commitment can lead to burnout. And burnout can happen not only with the leader but also with the congregation when one leader does everything. At first it seems wonderful to have someone willing to carry an overload, but eventually there is a burnout of followership.

Suggestions: Talk with Cynthia about her hopes and dreams for her life in the church. Help her to connect with her follower role as well as her leader role.

2. The Willing Leader

Jason will do anything you ask of him. No one has ever heard him say no. He would do everything if he could. He can be counted on to follow through on his commitments.

Positives: A person who says yes when asked to help is every recruiter's dream. A generous, willing spirit energizes others. A dependable person is valued.

Cautions: Is this person agreeing to do jobs he really can't do? Do the jobs fit his expertise and experience? Is he taking on tasks others could, and perhaps should, do?

Suggestions: Give Jason positive feedback. He is someone who wants to please.

Also enlist his ideas for passing jobs around. Make him part of an informal team to see that people in the church have opportunities to use their gifts and contribute to the whole.

3. The Entitled Leader

Henry has expressed his desire to be the church's moderator. He is faithful in church attendance. He has done many, many tasks around the church. He is not dynamic but is successful at most things he attempts.

Positives: Faithfulness is priceless. Breadth of experience is also a good thing.

Cautions: Don't immediately dismiss Henry as a possible leader. Some people may not have the dramatic "presence" of a Cynthia but can guide the ship with a steady hand. Ask, "What kind of leader do we need most at this moment in our life together?" There are times when we need Cynthia types and times when we need Henry types at the helm.

Suggestions: Henry may assume that he should be rewarded for his faithfulness by being asked to be the moderator. If he is needed more in another position, find other ways to recognize his faithful service both corporately and individually. Make sure he is genuinely appreciated for the jobs he does.

4. The Popular Leader

Iris is the Bible study teacher everyone wants to hear. She has a special gift for teaching and interpreting Scripture. In fact, she has led an adult Bible class for more than fifteen years.

Positives: Effective Bible teaching is a valuable asset to the congregation. Those who exercise the spiritual gift of teaching help build up the body of Christ.

Cautions: Get to know Iris's heart. She may yearn for different opportunities. Or she may fear doing other things. What other leadership roles might fit her gifts but be outside her usual niche? On the other hand, don't force her into other roles if this niche is truly the place where she is content and at her best.

Suggestions: Make sure Iris knows that jobs in the church are never lifetime appointments. Encourage Iris to periodically take time off from her teaching to rest or to serve in other venues.

5. The Discerning Leader

Russell has really come to life recently in the church. He understands the vision that is driving the ministry. He "gets" it. He connects with the concept of Immanuel—God with us.

Positives: The gift of discernment is a critical leadership quality. People who understand the driving vision and mission of the congregation and own it for themselves are essential.

Cautions: Owning the vision means buying into what the congregation has determined after a period of spiritual discernment. It does not mean controlling the vision but rather enabling the vision to blossom.

Suggestions: Propose that Russell communicate the vision to others in the congregation, thereby broadening the base of understanding. Encourage him to incorporate a variety of learning styles in his methods of communication in order to maximize congregational involvement. Work with him to establish a suitable timeline for the congregation to absorb and confirm the vision. Emphasize the value of listening both to the people and to God.

6. The Reluctant Leader

Muriel has recently completed a spiritual gifts study and now recognizes her spiritual gifts. Her findings have been affirmed by friends and family members. She knows the church as a place for her, but she isn't sure she should take an elected position at this point in her development.

Positives: Recognition of one's spiritual gifts is an essential step in leadership development. While Muriel's reluctance may be the result of shyness, it could also signal genuine humility and a teachable spirit. Leaders who know there is more to learn are likely to listen well. Humble leaders welcome opportunities for personal growth.

Cautions: Muriel may not only be new to the leadership arena but may also be new to the local church. Inviting her to serve in a key position to get her involved in the life of the church could inadvertently push her right out the "back door." Discover and evaluate the reason for her reluctance.

Suggestions: If Muriel simply needs some encouragement, consider arranging a mentorship in which her skills can be developed. Another approach may be to develop a team leadership position where she works with another person. Or offer her a position-elect slot where she can learn her job during the year prior to her election.

7. The "Limited" Would-Be Leader

Lacey is an extrovert with a winsome smile who wants to be a leader. She enjoys conversing with almost anyone. The problem is, as a person with mental limitations, she is not generally thought of as leadership material.

Positives: The church must treasure every part of the body of Christ. Lacey wants to give of herself. Her gift is one to be accepted.

Cautions: Don't let well-intentioned generosity tempt you to invite Lacey to accept a task that will set her up for failure. Likewise, don't place her where she will be the subject of negative observations.

Suggestions: Try to find a genuine place of service for Lacey that is within her capacity but doesn't seem like charity. Ask family members, caregivers, or others familiar with Lacey to advise you on her capacity. See if you can establish a job with a title. The solution might be in becoming the coffee hour hostess or in being a member of the usher team, with her job being to arrive at church a bit early and take the bulletins from the office to the back of the sanctuary for the ushers who will be seating people. Another possibility might be to find a specific task that she could handle within a current outreach ministry.

Be sure to thank Lacey regularly with specificity. For example, say, "Lacey, thank you for being part of the outreach team. I am grateful for your service in this church."

8. The "Wise" Leader

George has served in many leadership roles over the years. Now in his eighties, George would still like to be valued by the congregation. He remains active and mentally astute.

Positives: Someone who knows the territory is a positive asset. He is a seasoned leader with a long-term perspective.

Cautions: Is George able to catch the vision for the future? Find a job or advisory position that will tap his greatest strengths. If he does not own the vision, resist putting him in a place where he can veto plans for the future.

Suggestions: Honor age! Wisdom and age are not always synonymous, but both deserve respect. Many churches have established "emeritus" positions within boards and committees. Arguments can be made for and against this practice. If you do it, be sure the position has specific duties with boundaries.

9. The "Needy" Would-Be Leader

Derek has been through very difficult times. During his recovery, he has been touched by the love of the church. He wants to be a leader, but this desire comes from neediness more than from spiritual maturity.

Positives: The congregation often responds enthusiastically to a new convert or a person in some kind of recovery. Derek's testimony may be dramatically powerful.

Cautions: One of the biggest challenges in the church today is ministry with emotionally needy people. People come to the church for healing just as Derek did. For some, the process of healing feels so good that the individuals don't want to achieve health. They want to be the center of the healing ministry forever.

Suggestion: The best suggestion may be to involve Derek in some type of outreach ministry. His healing may come through serving. Service will also help develop Derek's leadership skills.

10. The "Less Than Enough" Leader

Beth's church boasts two retired seminary professors and three retired pastors. So this year, when the nominating committee asked

Beth to consider a key leadership position, her response was, "Not with those experts watching."

Positives: Beth has exhibited ability and willingness. She wants to do a good job with everything she attempts. She is not alone in coming to a task with less than enough time, experience, or courage.

Cautions: In a perfect church culture, Beth would not be the subject of criticism in her new leadership venture. However, if more experienced leaders tend to criticize rather than assist or encourage, Beth will need plenty of affirmation.

Suggestions: Jesus said of the woman who gave two coins, "She, with less than enough, has given all she had to live on" (Luke 21:4, NEB). Jesus honored the one who gave what she had.

Beth should be encouraged to give what she has. If she is open to entering into a mentorship, pair her with a retired professional or another experienced leader. Make sure she receives affirmation and encouragement.

Cultivating Leaders

Cultivating leadership is an organic process. We plant the seeds of leadership and watch them sprout. As growth occurs, we identify and develop new leaders. Then we rotate and recycle as needed. Cultivating leaders requires the repetitive routine of planting–growing–harvesting, planting–growing–harvesting over and over again.

Within every seed is the essence of life. When placed in the right environment—a nutritious mixture of soil, sunlight, and moisture—life bursts forth. Leadership development in the church mirrors this process. People are like plants. The church provides a healthy growing space.

People ready for leadership have already moved beyond the cold, dormant stage. They have displayed a willingness to grow. Enough sprouting has occurred that energy is evident. One can see the spark of life. Just as overwatering harms plants, so micromanagement overwhelms new leaders. On the other extreme, neglect in the form of no accountability and little support can cause promising leaders to wither. As in the case of reluctant Muriel, the challenge lies in finding ways to encourage "sprouters" without killing them.

Since not all leaders are alike, it follows that mass production of leaders is ineffective. While leadership training events are helpful, a one-size-fits-all approach is insufficient. We can plant the seeds of knowledge by providing training in the generalities of leadership, such as group theory, conflict management, and systems thinking. However, people don't grow into their full individual leadership roles in a class setting. A personalized approach is essential.

Some common gardening tips are easily applicable to the cultivation of the leadership pool.

Proper Placement

Experienced gardeners know that certain seedlings along with some established lackluster plants do better when they are moved to another location. Plants need the right growing conditions to thrive. Indirect sunlight might not be enough for a flowering perennial. Place it near a window and watch it produce a beautiful burst of color. Annual flower seedlings that spring up too close to each other remain spindly. Spread them out, and watch them flourish. Likewise, some plants furnish a showy display of color only when coupled with their complement. For example, placing silvery foliage beside vibrant red blossoms optimizes the appeal of both plants. Sometimes the placement problem manifests itself underground. Potted plants become root-bound. When this happens, the wise gardener moves them into larger containers or divides them into several smaller plants. Placement is crucial.

Leadership Application: People, like plants, have preferred conditions. With their unique strengths and characteristics, they do best when they are in the right growing space. Much like successful gardeners, leaders should tend to those with whom they serve. Moving, pairing, and mentoring are vital parts of the leadership cultivation process.

After we identify and place a leader, we may find ourselves disappointed with the person's performance. Applying the gardening tip about proper placement can help us improve the situation. Determine whether the leader is receiving nourishment. Does he need additional resources? How might you help provide them? Does she enjoy her role, or has she found that she would function better somewhere else? When could relocation take place? How can you assist in the meantime? Is there another person who could come alongside in a supportive role? What about providing a mentor? These are core questions to ask when you suspect a leader has been poorly placed.

Coaxing Growth

Some plants are finicky. They need to be coaxed to grow even in the right growing space. Some gardeners are better at this than others. We wistfully credit the successful one as having a "green thumb." Yet a little tender loving care produces visible benefits almost anywhere in the plant kingdom.

Leadership Application: Encouragement produces results. Discerning words of encouragement are highly motivational. Not all encouragement needs to be verbalized. Sometimes a supportive act is just as encouraging as well-spoken words. We'll say more about encouragement in chapter 7 when we highlight the church as a base for "burden-lifted leadership."

Crop Rotation

Farmers and gardeners know that certain crops begin to do poorly if the seeds are planted in the same ground year after year. For instance, the potato patch or cornfield needs to be relocated from time to time. If it isn't, the crop becomes diseased. Plants such as peas and beans return nutrients to the soil. When we rotate their growing spaces, other plants can take advantage of their predecessor's gifts.

Leadership Application: Rotate leadership. Most people don't want to be stuck in one leadership role forever. In fact, the perception that one's role will turn into a "forever" position often keeps people from even considering saying yes to a recruiter. Be creative as you look over the leadership needs in your church. Would more people be involved if they knew they were expected to serve for a relatively short time? If so, place reorganization on the table for discussion. How might present responsibilities be divided to remove the burden from the few and involve more people in leadership?

An attractive by-product of rotation is rest. Old Testament teachings come into play as we seek to cultivate leaders. Just as land was intended to be allowed to rest every seventh or sabbatical year, leaders ought to have prescribed rest as well. During the year(s) of rest, leaders explore and, ideally, find fulfillment in their roles as followers.

Consider the example of Elm Street Church. It has about two hundred members. It is healthy by most standards—steady or growing attendance, warm and joy-filled fellowship, vigorous Christian education. The church has two laypersons who are particularly good public speakers. These two men have become like associate pastors. One or the other of them almost always has a role in worship. When the congregation needs to select a moderator, they immediately think of these two as possible candidates. This situation is not bad. It is a blessing to have people like this in the congregation. The problem is that other people who could offer leadership hold back, assuming these two can do whatever needs to be done.

Elm Street had the wisdom to realize that they needed to find a way to get others involved without losing the giftedness of the two men. They instituted a rotational leadership philosophy. Simply stated, it reads, "In our church, we will seek to engage the gifts of all members. We encourage members to try a new task within the life of the church every three years."

While a plethora of print resources can be found on the subject of leadership, little is available on effective followership. As leaders rotate into followership, they frequently have difficulty mentally letting go of previous responsibilities. They may also struggle with what it means to be effective followers without unduly compromising the leader persona that has begun to flourish. Nevertheless, rotating leadership and followership is one of the most effective ways for churches to adapt to the needs of contemporary life.

Implementing the sabbath-year principle also enables an organization to deal more effectively with leadership dynasties. Every church has them, and they deter new leaders from using their God-given gifts. When we cultivate both followership and leadership, we discourage the rise of dynasties.

Deadheading and Pruning

If we expect plants to produce fruit and flowers, old blossoms and extraneous foliage, vines, and branches must be removed. Deadheading is tedious work, but plants respond by sending out glorious new blossoms. Pruning can be painful, not only to the plant, but also to the gardener. "Why remove all that healthy, luscious growth?" we ask. The plant responds by focusing its growth in fruit production.

Leadership Application: Help leaders with self-assessment. Churches are infamous for using people to keep the organization going. What if, instead, we became famous for helping people take an honest look at themselves and their roles? Are they doing too much? Are the multitalented and multigifted people doing everything? Are leaders just maintaining a machine, or are they engaged in ministry? What extraneous tasks could be removed so that more energy could be used to produce spiritual fruits?

Sadly, none of these suggestions for identifying and cultivating leaders will work if there are systemic root causes of the leadership crisis in your church. Dig deep to discover the issues. Is your church stuck in old patterns? Do you need to update job descriptions? Review the expectations of leaders in light of life's realities. Find out if people are saying, "Is this all there is?" Ask them, "Why?" and invite candid responses. Then listen carefully to what they say.

● ● ● ● ● ● ● ● ● ● ● ● ● ● ● ●

INGRID'S STORY

Are leaders born or made? The probable answer is "both." They are born and made. I was.

I was only five years old when my dad told me I should tone down my approach with the children in the neighborhood. Actually, he told me I was too bossy. But somebody had to organize them, and why shouldn't it be me? I took the role seriously. They didn't seem to mind, and we all had a good time together. Some might say I was a born leader.

During my school years, I was elected to the usual positions in classes, church youth groups, extracurricular interest groups, and our interdenominational youth council. My church, my schools, and my community were safe places for me to grow. My family, teachers, and pastors encouraged me and my friends. Together we were young leaders. It's just what we did.

It wasn't until I found myself in the role of minister's wife in my midtwenties that I actually began to think about my leadership role. When I was invited by my mentor to serve with her on a conference committee, I wondered what I could possibly have to offer among this group of older, more experienced women. I was both excited and hesitant as I went to my first meeting. I was surprised to learn that they accepted me as a peer and listened with interest to my meager suggestions. In addition to working together to plan a conference, we forged an informal mentor/mentee relationship by committee. Because of their care and encouragement, the door into statewide denominational women's ministry opened to me.

These women were making me a leader.

The situation was similar in our next pastorate. Through the women's ministry within that state, I was encouraged to take a position that introduced me to the national arena. I benefited from the personalized care of the executive director and sister members of the board. By participating in training events and subsequently accepting challenges to use what I had learned, I began to consider myself a leader.

When I applied the things I was learning, I began taking more confident steps. The baby steps had long since given way to an eager child's quick but sometimes faltering steps. The ensuing teenage years added some flamboyant steps, while young adulthood resulted in a measured, dependable gait. And so the pace was set. From time to time, I have had opportunities to walk alongside others to help them explore the path to leadership. Early identification and careful cultivation by many people through the years resulted in the growth of a leader.

● ● ● ● ● ● ● ● ● ● ● ● ● ● ● ● ●

QUESTIONS for Personal Reflection or Group Discussion
1. What do you consider to be your spiritual gifts?
2. How does a deeper understanding of spiritual gifts and fruits lead us to discover and develop new leaders?
3. How does your church provide a healthy growing space for people to use their God-given gifts and produce spiritual fruit?
4. What would happen in your church if the priorities focused on the growth of the individual instead of keeping the organization functioning?
5. Identify places where you need to apply the gardening principles of deadheading and pruning. How will you find the courage to implement them?
6. What makes a sabbath year effective?

Notes

1. Roger Fredrikson, *God Loves the Dandelions* (Waco, Texas: Word Books, 1975).

2. "New Gallup Book Destroys the Myth of the Well-Rounded Leader" (Gallup Press, December 23, 2008), http://www.gallup .com/press/113536/Press-Release-Strengths-Based-Leadership .aspx (accessed December 10, 2010).

CHAPTER 4

Christian Leaders on the Job

When a believer chooses to follow Christ in believer's baptism or confirmation, the pilgrimage as a disciple has begun. That pilgrimage requires prayer, study, worship, fellowship within the body of Christ, and faithful action in the world. Many struggle with what being a disciple means. Discipleship is not a nine-to-five job. Nor is it a Sunday nine-to-noon job. To become a disciple of Jesus Christ is to become totally committed to living as Christ would have us live.

God calls everyone to ministry. Regardless of the field to which God calls us—education, health care, civil service, politics, sales, manufacturing, or full-time parenting—that's our primary arena for service. And service is what ministry is all about.

In his letter to the Ephesians, Paul urged his readers to lead a life worthy of the calling to which they had been called (Ephesians 4:1, NRSV). Worthiness is fairly subjective, so Paul gave the Ephesians some hints. He told them to live "with all humility and gentleness, with patience, bearing with one another in love, making every effort to maintain the unity of the Spirit in the bond of peace" (vv. 2-3, NRSV). These elements are key to living a well-balanced, godly life.

The most effective church leaders are those persons whose balanced lives reflect their faith at home, in the church, and in the world. Unfortunately, many of us live fragmented lives. In our Ministry of the Laity in the Workplace resource, *Renewing God's People*,[1] we noted that people tend to exhibit one personality, value system, or attitude for business, another for family, and another for church. The concept of being faithful in every arena of life has been taught, but few of us have internalized it. Sadly, what is discussed at church often doesn't seem relevant to the challenges we face in the world of work.

This fragmented approach to Christian living is counterproductive. By demonstrating one personality at church, another at work, and yet another at home, we lose energy. The lack of wholeness drains us. In contrast, when we sincerely carry our faith into every part of our lives, we find greater energy. Our lives both in and outside the church become more dynamic when we have a faith that permeates every aspect of life. (Discover the "Seven Steps toward Personal Wholeness" that we suggest in chapter 6.)

Living one's faith in the world has been called "ministry of the laity." However, that phrase is often confused with lay ministry programs that train lay leaders to serve as clergy. Perhaps a better term is "ministry in daily life." How do Christians, and particularly persons with gifts for leadership in the church, carry their faith into every aspect of their lives?

What sounds plausible at church on Sunday may be tough to "live out" on Monday. We may *want* to reflect our faith in all our actions, but we find it difficult. Churches need to care about the daily ministry of their congregants. A healthy church is a vital refueling station, a place not only for education, but also for motivation. When the church serves as this refueling station, we are encouraged and challenged to *be* the church in every arena of life. We'll elaborate on the church's role as a refueling station in chapter 7. But now, let's take a closer look at Christian leaders who strive to carry their Sunday lessons into the Monday world.

Characteristics of Christian Leaders on the Job

Lutheran layman and retired steel industry executive William Diehl has written extensively on faith in the workplace. From *Thank God, It's Monday* to *The Monday Connection*, Diehl helped frame the ongoing conversation about discipleship. The following characteristics are based on his writing.[2]

They Do Their Work Well

Competency is the most basic level of ministry in daily life. People who do their work in the best way they can gain credibility with their coworkers. In chapter 2 we tried to imagine Joseph's excellent carpentry work. Likewise, we can speculate about the quality of tents Paul, Aquila, and Priscilla turned out (Acts 18:2-3). In any case, we believe their work reflected their faith and integrity.

Christians, of course, are not the only workers who strive for excellence in the workplace. But as Christians, we are motivated by the faith that guides our lives. We are good workers because of the one in whom we believe. Other people may be good workers for other reasons.

Don works in law enforcement. His on-the-job performance rating is high. He is quick to affirm that he employs the Golden Rule (Matthew 7:12) in his daily decision making. He chooses to look at both perpetrators and victims as people and believes that others realize his concern is legitimate. "It's something you can't fake," he says. Out of a position of strength, he chooses to be compassionate, understanding, and merciful. Don does his work well.

They Truly Care about Others

Good Christian leaders are open, sensitive, respectful, caring people. They are also good listeners. By displaying their genuine care in a variety of ways, they contribute to the well-being of those around them. In so far as possible, they work to establish a culture of caring in their workplace.

Kayleen knows little things make a big difference in the workplace. During the pre-Christmas rush of her first year of employment at an elder-care facility, she shopped for a gift to give a peer whose name she had drawn for the office gift exchange. After carefully selecting something appropriate, she thought perhaps she should buy a gift for her supervisor as well. Not knowing the office protocol, she hesitated and almost changed her mind. But she followed her initial instinct and bought her supervisor a small gift. When Kayleen gave it, her supervisor responded with tears. Kayleen believes that her inner nudging was from God because God knew her supervisor needed that extra loving expression of care and support. Kayleen nurtures a culture of caring in her workplace.

They Do the Right Thing

Ethical dilemmas confront us on all sides. We may be called on to make decisions that ultimately put pressure on our own job security or the effectiveness of our employing organization. As Christians, we are called to make good ethical decisions. In addition, we add value by continually examining the standards by which decisions are made.

Making the right decisions for the right reasons is a challenge. The mistake we often make is to decide without really thinking. We succumb to knee-jerk decision making. In our polarized political climate, we are tempted to agree with everything said by the politicians we like and disagree with everything said by the politicians we don't like. If we are honest with ourselves, we may be taken aback by listening carefully to someone from the "other" side. We may realize that in some instances we actually agree. No political party is right all the time. No preacher is right all the time. No one of us is right all the time. Careful, prayerful study of any situation can lead us to make better decisions. Coworkers and friends have greater regard for a leader who listens, thinks, and prays, and then arrives at a decision.

Anthony is a retired prison guard. In recalling his years working in the correctional system, he is quick to admit that as a Christian guard, he was pressed with countless challenges. For example, he asks, "Was I a positive Christian witness while I restrained a prisoner in a potentially violent setting? Most of the time it was a mere contest of the wills. I would have preferred some room for individual consideration." However, Anthony had plenty of opportunities to offer individual consideration to inmates who came to him with complaints. "They learned quickly that if they took a complaint to me, they would get attention," he notes. He was a conscientious listener. If inmates were mistaken and the complaints ill-founded, he showed them where they were wrong. If the complaints appeared to be valid, Anthony took the time to bring them to others who could help. Later he checked back with the originators of the complaints to make sure they were getting proper assistance. "As a Christian in the workplace, it was my job," Anthony asserts.

When Necessary, They Work for Change

Unjust systems change when individuals continually work for that change. While change itself is said to be constant, it tends to subtly overlook prejudicial behavior, discrimination, and other similarly unjust practices. People have to address the wrongs and effect changes that have the potential to right the wrongs. Fairness in the workplace remains a visionary goal, and Christian leaders are well-equipped to take the lead to bring it into reality.

Marie was an executive staff person in an organization with about three hundred employees. It was her job to bring to the leadership team recommendations for salary adjustments at the end of the year. Marie realized right away that, across the board, men received higher compensation than women. Instead of rising up in righteous indignation, Marie carefully studied both the compensation history and the current situation.

When the time came for her presentation to the team, she made recommendations that reflected comparative job responsibilities, experience, decision-making responsibilities, and other pertinent factors. The leadership team didn't implement all of her recommendations the first year. They didn't like facing the injustices in their system. But Marie's work was impeccable, and she stayed on task. She came back year after year, steadily pushing the system to a position of integrity. Marie was an effective change agent.

They Practice What They Preach

Healthy Christian leaders put their beliefs into action in their personal lives. In other words, they promote their personal brand in ways that inspire others to believe in it too. Those who say one thing and do another quickly disprove their brand, making it nothing but words. A Christian leader's lifestyle must consistently communicate deepest-held values.

Perhaps the biggest disconnect for Christians in the United States today is experienced in weighing our conspicuous consumption against New Testament teaching. It is easy for us to judge those economically above us, but we have yet to give serious thought to the reality of our own affluence compared to the majority of the world's population. There isn't an easy answer. For many of us, moving away from the materialism of our culture is a lifelong process.

As an administrator at a major southern university, Evelyn was responsible for human resources' compliance with laws and university procedures. Her job was always challenging, but during a particularly difficult time, the pressure was on in direct and indirect ways for her to flex more than she knew was right. The situation was intricate, involving numerous legal and ethical issues. The consequence of not flexing could have been the loss of her job. Moreover, there was also the possibility of the university losing a significant amount of money. Evelyn had to continually make her case before the president of the university and other administrators, some of whom believed she was misguided and unrealistic. This particular crisis lasted for months and took a heavy emotional toll on all involved.

During this time, Evelyn began to confide in her pastor, and she was able to find strength in her faith. Her commitment to the rights of the "least of these" was a driving force. In the end, Evelyn was vindicated in her position. She continued in her job, fighting for the rights of all. As Evelyn practiced what she preached, her relationship with her church family grew stronger than it had ever been.

They Tell the Story at the Right Time

Individuals who practice the first five leadership principles in this list will undoubtedly find themselves with the opportunity to share their faith with others. Sometimes we feel uncomfortable talking about our faith. Our discomfort may occur because we have run into people in the past who have been obnoxious, pushing their particular beliefs at us. A person who "lives" faith in the manner suggested in the previous characteristics will experience natural moments when people ask them faith questions. At those moments, they will be able to share the power of their personal relationship with Jesus Christ.

Faith sharing can even happen in a public school classroom. Mike recalls his years as a middle school teacher. He was teaching a unit on home and family when a student asked him if he went to church. After Mike acknowledged that he did, the student said, "I don't get it. You don't seem like a religious person." When Mike asked the student to clarify his statement, the student responded, "Well, you smile, you have fun, and you're hardly ever grumpy. How can you be religious and not look sad all the time?" At that point, Mike was able to explain in general terms that being religious is not synonymous with a despondent attitude. The students listened attentively as he shared part of his personal story in the applicable context of his own childhood family setting. That interactive class session opened doors for him with his students because he was willing to tell his story.

Workplace Witness Impacts Local Church Ministries

The people who go to church *are* the church. The church is the people of God. Therefore, during the week, 99 percent of a church's ministries take place outside the physical walls of its Sunday morning gathering site. The church deploys to the workplace on Monday morning. There most congregants face demanding situations. Their integrity is regularly placed on the line. Their ethics are challenged. They ask, and are often forced to answer, hard questions. In answer to the challenges the workplace presents, Christian leaders are encouraged to respond with humility, gentleness, patience, and love. How then do these leaders impact the ministry of the institutional church?

The local church does not exist in a terrarium. In a closed ecosystem such as a terrarium, the environmental conditions are controlled. The humidity is just right. There is no wind. Lighting and heating systems are added to meet the needs of the life forms growing inside. Plants are totally protected.

Local churches aren't that fortunate; they are fully exposed to the elements. They can't minister effectively if they don't have concrete connections to the world. Those connections are most often made through the lives of the congregants. While a particular church makes weekly connections with a given number of people, the congregants themselves connect with many, many more every day of the week. Healthy church leaders and the church itself benefit from these day-to-day connections in the world. The practice of our faith informs the way we interact in the world, and those interactions with the world in turn inform the practice of our faith. To further understand the impact of these connections, consider their context, focus, and relevance.

Context

Engagement with both the workday world and the church provides church leaders with a context. Christ's call to discipleship doesn't come in a vacuum. We live in the world, and that's where our discipleship will be most often demonstrated. From this context, leaders come to the institutional church expecting the body of Christ to respond to the realities of the real world.

All too often, the teaching church has been silent on the subject of the church at work, focusing instead on church work. Christian leaders yearn for a balanced approach, where the sacred and secular unite. When Sunday lessons affirm each person's call to ministry and help congregants connect their faith with daily life and work, the church's Monday impact will be distinct.

Focus

A local church's engagement in the world enables that particular body of Christ to develop a specific focus for ministry. Most congregations desire to be "full-service churches," but it is becoming increasingly more important for them to discern their two or three primary means of outreach. These means in turn form the identity of that congregation. In the process of discernment, the members will bring all their experiences of ministry in their daily lives to bear on the decision.

First Church, a downtown church in a medium-sized city, had existed for well over one hundred years with a self-image that suggested prestige and position. The surprising thing was that this church also had a truly welcoming spirit. A woman in a beautiful fur coat sat in the same pew with a man who looked as though he had slept in a dumpster, and no one seemed to mind! The woman was not ill at ease, and neither was the man. The church came close to practicing inside its doors what was preached from the pulpit.

A new pastor came and realized the church's ministry was limited to its building. The fact that he lived in the neighborhood provided him with a stunning reality check that he put to good use. Slowly he began to educate. He sought out key leaders who could catch the vision. Little by little the church began to look beyond its property.

The first big change came when a number of churches in that part of the city conducted a needs survey. As a result, they discovered a dramatic need for hot meals on Saturdays. First Church offered to be the host church. While all the churches in the area helped provide food, the meals were served at First. This action was simply the beginning. As the church continues to connect with the world outside its doors, it continues to progress to full discernment of its unique ministry for this time.

Relevance

Engagement with both the world and the church provides opportunities to perform reality checks. Pastors and teachers wish to be relevant. They want to present content that helps congregants *be* the church. When Sunday's lessons and sermons are prepared through the lenses of the people in the pew, the church's teaching and preaching ministries can be more effective.

For vision through the laity lens to be clear, intentional diaogue and mutual accountability are essential. Christian leaders help create ways to encourage meaningful clergy/laity conversation. This can take place during feedback sessions and workplace visitations and in one-on-one settings. In these types of scenarios, participants establish trust, which is key to mutual accountability.

Pastor Theresa wanted to have a better sense of the workplaces of her congregation. It couldn't be done in every situation, but where possible, she arranged a visit to each person's workplace. She would sit somewhere quietly and simply watch the work being done.

One of her most memorable visits was to the restaurant where Mattie was a server. While Mattie's boss agreed to the visit, he declared that sitting in a booth wouldn't give the pastor the full picture. He invited Theresa to spend half her time in a booth and the other half on a stool in a corner of the kitchen during the noon rush. "I had an idea what to expect," said Theresa, "but it went far beyond my imagination. Seeing Mattie doing her work helped me understand much more about her and the place she spends so much of her time. I'm not at all sure I could keep up with Mattie." Later conversations between Mattie and Theresa were deeper and richer because Theresa had at least a little exposure to one of the places where Mattie carries out her ministry in daily life.

Healthy churches recognize the widespread ministries of their members. They acknowledge and affirm the every-part-of-life discipleship that members are seeking to live. Such a church rejoices in the ways its congregation is having an impact across the community. Such a church also provides opportunities for study and growth groups that talk about daily life ministry.

Churches that have a solid understanding of the ministry of each member find they gain a new perspective on leadership. The leaders who emerge in this kind of church are persons who see the wide context of the church's ministry and want to engage in encouraging and facilitating it.

For Personal Reflection or Group Discussion

1. What daily challenges do you face as a disciple of Christ?
2. In his letter to the Ephesians, Paul urged his readers to lead a life worthy of the calling to which they had been called (Ephesians 4:1, NRSV). What does this mean to you? Why?
3. In what ways is your church a refueling station?
4. In our competitive, fragmented world, how can the church help you find balance?
5. What criteria do you use to make right decisions for the right reasons?
6. What has been your response to unfairness in the workplace?
7. What difference does your faith make in your daily life?

Notes

1. Susan Gillies and Ingrid Dvirnak, *Renewing God's People: The Design Guide* (Valley Forge, PA: National Ministries, American Baptist Churches, USA, 1992), 5.

2. William E. Diehl, *Thank God, It's Monday* (Philadelphia: Fortress, 1982). The first five characteristics of "Christian Leaders on the Job" are based on ideas first presented by William E. Diehl. See his book *The Monday Connection: On Being an Authentic Christian in a Monday–Friday World* (San Francisco: Harper, 1991), 23, 57, 83, 109, 137. Some of the illustrations are loosely based on interviews we conducted as we prepared to write *Renewing God's People.*

CHAPTER 5

Linked Leadership

What is the business plan of most churches? Isn't it essentially to make disciples, baptize, and teach people to do what Jesus said to do? The church's mission is to carry on Jesus' ministry. Of course, the ways in which the mission is carried out vary from church to church.

The cattle rancher in Nebraska also has a business plan. Simply put, it is to sell beef. To succeed, the rancher makes the health of the herd a primary concern. The rancher ensures that the cattle are fed and cared for. But essential to the operation is the crop of new calves. The rancher implements ideas and strategies to help each calf come into the world safely, eat well, grow, and stay healthy. The rancher has no chance of fulfilling this business plan if he or she focuses only on how many cows are taken to market. Developing the new generation is absolutely essential.

So it is in a healthy church. The church has a vision for what it wants to be. To reach that vision, the church is concerned about the health of the whole family. When children, youth, singles, seniors, or any others in the family become a distant sideline of the church's mission, the body suffers. To have a healthy body, the church needs good leaders. Good leaders are developed as healthy people who integrate into the total ministry of the church. Generating leaders is part of the church's ministry.

The question for healthy churches today is, what is the best way to engage everyone in the congregation in ministry? The congregation is made up of all kinds of people and personality types. One size never fits all. So how does a church become a living body, celebrating all of its various parts and working together for good?

Teach Children to Lead

The greatest leaders may have unique leadership gifts, but for the majority of persons who assume leadership roles, leading is a learned skill. Training even young children for leadership, if done carefully, can bless the children and the congregation.

Kudos to all those women and men who have directed Sunday church school Christmas pageants! At their worst, the pageants traumatized some of the child performers, uncovered some of the worst of parental competition, and distracted the congregation from the meaning of Christmas. At their best, they helped children discover the joy of telling the Christmas story through drama, experience the delight of doing something they never thought they could do, and blessed a congregation by reminding them of the awesome God of the universe coming to earth as a baby.

Many pastors and lay leaders can remember their first experiences of stepping forward from the group to say a line in a Christmas pageant. And that first leadership moment was usually followed by affirmation from members of the congregation. In our experience, the majority of people develop much more readily in the light of affirmation and encouragement rather than in negative feedback. What sort of feedback are we giving the children among us?

Whether intentionally or unintentionally, parents influence their children to be either leaders or followers. In some families, children are taught that they can accomplish anything on which they set their sights. They are encouraged to be leaders; they encounter positive role models. They are prompted to be active and to reject passivity. In other families, children are taught to be followers. When they become too assertive, they are admonished. Parents encourage and reward compliance. If these children encounter leaders and other positive role models, they come to view them as people whom they are content and even eager to follow.

In the church school classroom, teachers usually emphasize the need for children to follow. Obviously, a teacher's ultimate goal is to teach a child to follow Jesus. But how is that done most effectively? Too often teachers overemphasize the need to have children operate in a passive manner within the classroom. They reward compliance and give negative feedback when a child steps out of line, either literally or figuratively.

While we believe that the church needs followers as well as leaders, we also believe that teachers do a disservice to children by consistently relegating them to the role of follower. Teachers cannot accept disrespectful behavior, yet they can encourage resourcefulness. Ingenuity and imagination are valued leadership characteristics to be cultivated wherever they sprout. Teachers do not want to encourage attitudes of superiority or arrogance, but they do well to nurture self-confidence in the children. Effective teachers recognize that an orderly classroom enhances learning, but excessive discipline can foster feelings of powerlessness, apathy, and resentment in some children.

Most of us who grew up in a church are able to name one or more of our early childhood church school teachers. As we look back, we find teachers who exerted great influence on our young lives. They were our role models. They were the persons we pretended to be as we played "Sunday school" with our stuffed animals, siblings, or neighborhood friends. They were among the persons we aspired to become later in life. Teachers of children play a vital role in generating leaders.

Intentional leader development among children requires three key behaviors:

■ *Respect each person.* The easiest way to show respect is to listen. Not listening is a sign of disrespect. More than twenty years ago, there was a surge of interest in teaching listening skills. Churches began to hold training sessions. People discovered the lessons learned translated extremely well into home life and business life.

■ *Provide safe opportunities.* The familiar *Peanuts* comic strip has humorously depicted the nervousness many children feel when participating in a Christmas pageant. Some nervousness is just fine. It is a part of hoping to do well. Some children, however, are not ready for performance as soon as others. It may be wise to start by inviting the children to share a story with a guest who comes into the children's classroom. In this case, the children feel safe in their own setting but begin to experience what it is like to be up front.

■ *Give honest affirmation.* Giving someone affirmation produces a positive effect in the same way a grow lamp affects a plant. The grow lamp provides exactly the kind of light the plant needs, and the plant thrives in its glow. Try simple, honest comments such as these:

> "Thanks for reading the Scripture. You have a
> wonderful voice."
> "I think you should consider becoming a preacher."
> "I always love to see you up front helping with worship."

These kinds of comments are easy to make. They are also profoundly encouraging to a child. When you can't find something positive to say about what the child did, try a comment such as, "Thank you so much. I love the fact that you shared with us."

Opportunities to involve children in the life of the congregation extend beyond the Christmas pageant. Children can learn to lead when adults take the time to create teaching moments. The passion of a child who helps pack food baskets for those in need is infectious. The smile on the acolyte's face communicates delight. The eagerness of the junior usher signals a desire to do the job well. The innocence in the voice of a young reader not only refreshes and renews everyone who hears the reading of the Word but also reminds us of the One whom all of God's children are called to follow.

Teach Youth to Lead

Healthy congregations offer multitudes of opportunities for teenagers to learn leadership roles. The key word is *learn*. We do not develop effective leaders by simply dropping youth (or anyone else, for that matter) into leadership roles for which they have not been prepared. How can we best teach youth to lead?

Youth programs in churches span a wide spectrum of styles. The least effective are programs that have the youth sit and listen to an adult talk to them for the entire session. Adult leadership is critical. Teaching is critical. But the better methodologies engage the youth in the process. While the suggestions in the previous children's section also apply to youth, we highlight three additional components:

■ *Establish trust.* In order to teach youth to lead, their teachers, mentors, and leaders must be trustworthy. Trust is key to any successful relationship. If we want to teach youth to be trustworthy, we must first be trustworthy ourselves. We build trust when we are honest and reliable. As we lead by example, youth are more likely to welcome our guidance.

■ *Create partnerships.* Teaching youth to lead requires the creation of partnerships. Adults function as coaches rather than dictators. They help youth identify necessary roles and responsibilities. They encourage and support. They teach and model specific skills. Youth, in turn, gain a sense of empowerment and ownership as they share in decision-making processes.

■ *Complete meaningful tasks.* Youth learn to lead when they engage in meaningful tasks. Young people are capable and energetic. Whether raking leaves for the homebound or singing at a retirement home, youth want to make a difference in the world. When they plan and carry out worthwhile projects, they gain confidence, build competence, and look forward to further opportunities to serve.

These further service opportunities sometimes include teaching younger children. It is, however, a big mistake to hand a teenager a teacher's guide and ask him or her to teach third-grade Sunday school without any further direction. (This is a mistake when done with adults as well!) Inviting teens to help with younger children and to move into teaching by presenting part of a lesson is a good way to begin. Teens can grow into the role if it suits them, later teaching an entire unit. The regular teacher's mentoring role here is central to developing leaders.

When adults who teach youth recognize that the youth have something to teach them as well, wonderful growth can occur at all levels. In an age of social networking, there are seniors who feel technology has passed them by. Often when teens try to teach their grandparents or great-grandparents how to use the computer or access a social networking site, the youth move at a pace that leaves a grandma's head spinning. A little guidance in how to teach creates new possibilities for intergenerational connections.

At Central Community Church, the youth formed tech teams to assist seniors. (The senior adults often contributed to the fund-raising efforts for the youth mission trip, but the help of a tech team was not conditional on contributions.) Two of the wise elders asked a tech team to help them prepare several computer-generated presentations for a study group. The topics included, "Who Is My Neighbor?," which was based on the story of the good Samaritan. Interwoven into the study were complex issues of immigration. The Tech Team helped prepare the text and graphics for the slides and inserted video segments into the presentation. Once the work was completed, the senior study group invited the entire youth group to come see the completed presentations. The resulting discussion surprised both the youth and the seniors.

A church might offer a workshop or one-time class session on contemporary music as a snapshot of current culture. Have the youth teach it. Help the youth understand that the volume will have to be set at what may seem to them a ridiculously low level. The words will need to be copied for the adults or put on a screen. Invite the youth to talk about contemporary themes in music and how that differs from what was popular five years ago. Perhaps the youth have ideas about what they expect in the future. Encourage the adults to fully participate, ask questions, and show respect for the knowledge the youth have.

The involvement of youth in the life of the congregation goes far beyond the annual Youth Sunday. It even goes beyond the token membership slot on the advisory council. Invite and value their insights. Welcome their participation in congregational work and festive events. Recognize and celebrate their academic and extracurricular accomplishments. Ask them to solve technical dilemmas. Involve them as worship leaders, musicians, lay readers, ushers, and technicians. All along the way, be available to coach them in the techniques they may not yet know, and always be open to learn from them.

Teach Parenting

How will they learn if no one teaches them? The reality television show *Supernanny*, in which a British nanny came to a home and taught the parents how to be parents, was a success for several seasons. Why would this make an interesting reality show? Probably because so many people don't even know there are specific skills that can be learned in order to be more effective parents.

Parenting has become an accidental practice in our society, and dysfunctional family characteristics have been passed down from generation to generation. Children and parents together are sucked into a downward spiral because of the lack of good examples to follow. Moreover, demanding lifestyles drain many parents of any resources they may have had to nourish their children. The church has both the opportunity and responsibility to encourage personal, family, and congregational wholeness. One way this is accomplished is by teaching parenting skills.

There is no shortage of parenting program materials. Sessions include information on stress management, positive reinforcement, communication skills, setting behavioral goals and objectives, age-appropriate expectations, problem-solving skills, Internet awareness—the list goes on and on. The church that partners with parents becomes a refuge where people gather for support and instruction.

The church can also support and equip people for the next stage of parenting—grandparenting. Grandparents populate a variety of scenarios. Some are charged with raising their grandchildren. Others have long-distance relationships, while some are fortunate to live near their grandchildren. Whatever the situation, grandparents have unique opportunities to interact with children in influential ways.

The number of grandparents who are raising their grandchildren grows each year. The reasons are many, but common in each of the resulting households is the stress factor. They face overwhelming legal, financial, social, educational, and custodial challenges, and as a consequence, they are denied some of the joy commonly associated with the grandparent/grandchild relationship. Nevertheless, raising grandchildren can be rewarding. The church enhances the experience by coordinating community-wide support groups and instructional workshops.

Adults in long-distance relationships with their children and grandchildren are often lonely. In spite of the countless ways they are able to keep in touch, they may yearn for face-to-face interaction with the younger generation. Likewise, there are children in the church who live far away from their own grandmothers and grandfathers. Why not encourage surrogate relationships? Work with parents to form a mutually beneficial network of available seniors and children. Orient the adults on appropriate activities and procedures. Host a party to introduce the seniors and children to one another. (In keeping with recognized church safety regulations, employ the two-adults-present rule at all times.) Group activities will put both children and seniors at ease as they explore new rewarding relationships. Are there children in the church who attend worship or other activities without their parents? Engage friendly grandparent types to assist with these children. Help them feel that they are part of the family.

Too often we assume that adults who see their grandchildren regularly have been equipped to fill the role of grandmother or grandfather. After all, they attend countless games and school programs. They strengthen bonds by participating in birthday parties, hosting overnight visits, and including children in special outings. But that's not all there is to being a grandparent. Ideally, grandparents are positive role models who share their wisdom and experience in loving, caring ways. They help set the stage for grandchildren to move up the generational ladder. There are many resources to use to teach grandparenting skills. The church can help adults maximize their experiences by offering a "Grandparenting 101" class with refresher courses as needed.

Cultivate a Sense of Family

At the moment of believers' baptism in some churches and confirmation of baptism in others, the child is usually thought to become a member of the church. In some churches, the newly baptized young person becomes a voting member, and in others voting privileges come at a later age. It is important for congregations to provide age-appropriate opportunities for participation in the life of the church. Membership should have accompanying responsibilities. Being baptized or confirmed makes a difference in the young person's relationship to the congregation, and this difference should be recognized, celebrated, and concretized.

The church can develop strategies for providing quality opportunities for children and youth to gain leadership experience. Keep the opportunities in the context of the whole family. In other words, rather than creating artificial situations in which the children and youth are on display, integrate them into the life of the entire congregation.

There are times when children and youth can participate as worship leaders and serve as adjuncts or members-in-training on boards and committees. But perhaps the more creative strategies include a temporary children's committee or youth think tank in which particular questions or issues can be discussed and resolved. A word of warning here—don't give a youth think tank a question if you don't intend to follow their advice.

Ask young people to write items for the church newsletter or website. Give clear and specific story assignments. Be prepared to help them succeed.

Provide opportunities for interaction among the pastor, church leaders, children, and youth. Listen to their concerns and ideas. Work with them to achieve mutually satisfying results.

A child's faith development is everyone's responsibility. Just as it takes a village to raise a child, it takes the whole church family to help a child develop his or her faith. The healthy church does not simply relegate children and youth ministry to paid staff persons. A highly qualified paid staff is a tremendous blessing, but these persons should not be the only ones in the church with a sense of responsibility for the training of children and youth. The church can teach members how to be "church aunts and uncles." These are the encouragers. They make it a practice to affirm children in the church every time they see a child do something well (or even approaching "well").

United Church in a small midwestern city has about seventy-five members who possess a sense of family. One member says, "When I'm about to give up on my kids, we walk into that church and I know there will be people who will wrap those kids up in love when I've been ready to give them away!" Another member remembers that it took her more than a year after she joined the church to figure out which children belonged to which parents.

Children in that church may sit with their families in worship or sit with other families. Children are often seen before and after worship engaged in conversation with adults who are not related to them.

The church resettled a refugee family from Vietnam. The grandmother of the family was Buddhist and spoke no English but attended worship out of a sense of appreciation for what the church had done for her family. At the end of worship each Sunday, as the grandmother sat in a rear pew, someone would drop a baby in her lap while the parent tended to other business. The grandmother always had a baby in her lap but not always the same baby! She was delighted. The other children of the church watched this grandmother being a grandmother and accepted her as their "church grandma" as well.

Remember That Singles Are Part of the Family

It isn't hard to find single persons who have felt marginalized in their church. One forty-one-year-old businesswoman said, "In my church, it's really clear that everyone is much more excited when a family joins than when a single person joins." This woman wasn't so much angry with the church as she was frustrated by its response to singles. "Since I became a member, I've served on boards and committees, I've helped with special events, and my financial gifts are significant. Still, I feel 'extra.'"

The challenge of singles ministry is to maintain a balance between giving a unique focus to the specific ministry and simply incorporating single members into the body. A woman in an extremely large community church said that she was leaving her church because she was tired of being treated as "a broken whole." She felt her church saw singles as one part of a broken couple. The image of a church being composed of nuclear families—complete with Dad, Mom, boy child, and girl child—is no longer the norm. Single-parent families are a larger part of congregations than ever before.

Singles and single-parent families have a vital role to play in the ministry of the church. They are not unfortunates who are solely recipients of ministry any more or less than any other demographic group in the church. They want to be visible and dynamic but not set apart.

One denominational speaker reported going into a church to talk with the singles group. He did a presentation on how to get involved in outreach ministry. He said, "The reaction surprised me. They just stared at me. They were polite, but I knew something was wrong. It wasn't until afterward that I realized what was going on." This particular group had always seen themselves as persons to whom ministry should be extended. They had never been called forth to serve. The healthy church helps singles connect within the church family and community.

Find Creative Ways to Engage the Tired and Retired

Pastors often tell congregants, "You can't retire from kingdom work." But, in fact, people do. People retire because they are tired or because their lifestyles change. Some have served in a position for many years and feel it is time to let someone younger do it. In chapter 3, we highlighted some benefits of observing sabbath years. Everyone requires rest. When service opportunities are fluid enough to allow people to move between leadership and followership, workers are energized.

When healthy rotation is *not* practiced, burnout occurs. How might the church reengage the person who has experienced burnout? In some cases, it is impossible. The "been there, done that" attitude rules, and nothing you say will tempt the person to reconsider. However, if the opportunity is short-term, project-oriented, possibly shared with another, and appropriately suited to the individual, some people will respond positively.

Short-term, project-oriented opportunities also attract retirees. When people retire from their employed positions, many retire from their leadership positions in the church at the same time. A sense of freedom overtakes new retirees. They want to operate on their own schedule. After they enjoy their long-awaited getaways, many return to some sort of routine. Although the typical elected positions may not appeal to them, retirees remain gifted people who have time to give to kingdom work. Work with retirees to create attractive, individualized opportunities.

Retired clergy and their spouses comprise a subcategory of retirees. While retired clergy will always be clergy, retirement suddenly morphs them into the laity category of a church. In retirement, they abruptly join the people in the pew. This transition can be unsettling. Today's retired clergy person is the same gifted individual who led a congregation last year. The only difference is age. After a well-deserved rest, these retirees sometimes engage in interim ministries. Others do not. Creative, short-term, specialized approaches to leadership can help retired clergy (and often their spouses) reengage.

Once again, affirmation and appreciation are key. Retirees no longer receive affirmation from an employer and coworkers. In some cases, their spouse has died. Adult children are occupied with their own lives. The energy it takes to express appreciation for a job well done is minimal. The rewards are innumerable.

Leadership Links
In the healthy church, everyone is a link in the leadership chain. If the chain appears to be missing a link, rest assured that it is

only unidentified, disengaged, or underdeveloped. As we intentionally include and empower everyone, we repair and strengthen the chain.

Much of what has been said in this chapter appears in age-specific contexts. However, many guidelines for developing the leadership characteristics in children apply to youth and adults as well, and vice versa. There are people in every church today who feel they don't have a voice. Encouragement, opportunity, and affirmation will make a difference.

Today's church leaders can find encouragement for kingdom work in Paul's words to the Ephesians:

> The gifts [Christ] gave were that some would be apostles, some prophets, some evangelists, some pastors and teachers, to equip the saints for the work of ministry, for building up the body of Christ, until all of us come to the unity of the faith and of the knowledge of the Son of God, to maturity, to the measure of the full stature of Christ.... Speaking the truth in love, we must grow up in every way into him who is the head, into Christ, from whom the whole body, joined and knit together by every ligament with which it is equipped, as each part is working properly, promotes the body's growth in building itself up in love. (4:11-13, 15-16, NRSV)

QUESTIONS for Personal Reflection or Group Discussion

1. What opportunities for leadership do children and youth have in your church?
2. How are people incorporated into the life and ministry of your church?
3. What elements in your church's culture nurture the faith and leadership development of children?
4. If you grew up in a church, how did you experience the

encouragement of "church uncles, aunts, and grandparents"? In what ways can you help the children and youth in your church to become effective disciples?

5. How might your church help prevent burnout among leaders?

6. In what ways could your church engage retirees in short-term ministries?

7. How does your church fully engage singles as part of the healthy whole?

CHAPTER 6

How Do I Make It Fit?

Effective leadership demands personal wholeness. People move toward personal wholeness by balancing professional, personal, and domestic responsibilities. Healthy Christians integrate faith and daily life, establishing and maintaining relationships that heal, encourage, and challenge. They experience the biblical concept of *shalom*.

The Hebrew word *shalom* encapsulates both the hope and the reality of wholeness, not only for the individual, but also for society and the entire world. The verb form of the word literally means to make whole or complete. The noun form denotes a state of wholeness. When used to greet or say farewell to someone, the word communicates a deeper meaning than a simple hello or good-bye. *Shalom* is a rich blessing! In many circles, *shalom* is also equated with peace, but it encompasses much more than that. Along with the meanings already listed, *shalom* suggests completeness, fullness, well-being, health, and harmony. It is the very essence of all we seek.

What further inspires us to embark on a journey toward wholeness? Eugene Peterson's *The Message* renders Jesus' words in Matthew 5:48 in this way: "Grow up. You're kingdom subjects. Now live like it. Live out your God-created identity. Live generously and graciously toward others, the way God lives toward you" (MSG). Even in nonbiblical writings, historians referred to Jesus' teachings. One quoted Jesus as calling for wholeness when he said, "If you bring forth what is within you, what you bring forth will save you. If you do not bring forth what is within you, what you do not bring forth will destroy you."[1] Our God-given identity, that which lies deep within, must emerge and thrive.

It sounds well and good to live a life of wholeness—a life in which one's personality and faith expression are the same at home, at work, and at church. But how does it work? Too many people live lives that are filled but not necessarily *fulfilled*. The majority don't even have time to think about moving toward personal wholeness. Instead, *stress* and *coping* have become common words in their vocabulary. Everyone is too busy. Life goes faster and faster. Today's society deems workaholics to be people who are dedicated and worthy of honor instead of people who have unbalanced their lives often to a point of spiritual bankruptcy.

Spiritual health as well as the process involved in seeking it can result in a more efficient and integrated life. Stress drains energy, while exercising wholeness focuses energy. Spiritually healthy leaders find it possible to come to terms with the stresses of life in a gracious manner. They develop an appropriate perspective on life. Coping becomes a refined skill.

Spiritual health favorably impacts mental and physical health too. As we focus inward on our God-given identity, our mental health improves. We begin to base our security on who we are and who we are becoming rather than on what we do, what we have, or what others think of us. Because we are complex beings, our mental health affects our physical health and vice versa. For example, unchecked stresses can manifest themselves as physical maladies. Likewise, a primary focus on physical challenges may play out in some level of depression. Indeed, spiritual health impacts all of life. The more authentic we become, the more effective we find ourselves to be. Who we are at our very core affects every arena of life.

It follows, then, that church leaders are most effective and offer the most to the body (and to themselves) when they are spiritually healthy. In a healthy church, we—the congregants—bring all of who we are to the body of Christ. And myriad things happen. As a part of this fellowship, through worship, education, and interaction with others, we grow in spiritual health. As we grow, we begin to realize that our desire to serve is greater than our need to receive. As we give and serve, study and worship, we have the potential to grow to a deeper spiritual level than we would have thought possible.

Steps on the Journey

Are you ready to begin this journey toward wholeness? Carefully consider the seven basic steps that follow. As you do so, realize that the process may take a few days or several months. Ultimately, this journey lasts a lifetime. It will work best if you set aside specific time to work on the individual steps. You may want to find an accountability partner and regularly report your progress. It is a good idea to document your process in a journal or special computer file.

Seven Steps toward Personal Wholeness

1. Find the faith value in your daily life.
2. Find a theme Scripture for your ministry in daily life.
3. Find or establish a faith-connection group.
4. Explore what you can do to strengthen your faith community.
5. Seek balance.
6. Honor your work.
7. Study and practice the spiritual disciplines.

Find the Faith Value in Your Daily Life

Do you recognize the ways your faith permeates your entire life? A good place to begin evaluating the way you see your faith and life working together is to take a look at the faith value of your work.

"Work" is the place where you invest a significant amount of your energy. For most people, it is the place of employment, but it may also be a place where you serve as a volunteer or the home in which you invest most of your time. Begin by asking yourself which of the following two questions you consider to be primary:

1. Is my job a part of the way I live out my faith?
2. Is my job a financial resource so that I can live out my faith in other ways?

Finding the faith value in your daily life will seem simple if you work in one of the traditional helping professions: health care, education, counseling, social work, life coaching, or pastoral ministry. But even if you are not involved in a helping profession, what you do contributes to the common good. For example, if you work in a service or manufacturing industry, you are obviously meeting an expressed need. If you determine that the purpose of your work is only to fund other projects of worth, spend some time in reflection to see if you can identify spiritual meaning and additional purpose in the nature of the work itself.

Leah is a realtor who finds her work a way to serve people in transition. She says that when people are looking for a new home, it is usually because they are in some phase of transition. A family may be moving to a new community, which means they have had to leave another. People often buy homes because their life situation has changed. A move may be necessary to accommodate a growing family or to adjust to being empty nesters. Leah finds her ministry to be serving people in transition.

Jerry works in a convenience store. The challenge he has given himself is to try to set a positive tone for each early morning customer. His words of encouragement have drawn people to his store. Many come each day for a dose of Jerry's joy. It is not unusual for a customer to ask Jerry how he manages to be the way he is. His usual response is simply, "Jesus loves me." Jerry's employer wouldn't want him pulling out a Bible at the cash register, but Jerry knows a seed has been planted each time he responds in this manner.

Al is in the roofing business. In the city where he works, roofers have a bad reputation. Some dishonest roofers got in trouble, and the resulting publicity has made all roofers suspect. Al keeps his focus clear. "We believe in safe shelter for families," he says, "and our part is doing the very best job of roofing we can do." People who know him can see evidence of his faith in the way he conducts himself at home and on the job as well as at church.

An old, old story used in many sermon illustrations now ricochets around the Internet via e-mail. In the story, a traveler happens on a building site where a number of stonecutters are working. He asks three of them what they are doing. "I'm cutting stones," the first man replies. "It's mindless work, but I need the money." The second worker says, "I'm the best stonecutter working here." Pointing to a pile of building materials at his side, he urges, "Look at those smooth edges. You can't beat that!" The third man seems to be doing the same thing as the first two. He points at the foundation several yards away and says, "I'm building a cathedral." All three are doing the same task, but only one has placed his work in its larger, value-based perspective.

Find a Theme Scripture for Your Ministry in Daily Life

Finding a theme Scripture can be an enjoyable process of exploration, study, and even revelation. Take some time to recall Bible passages that have particularly touched you and seem to fit the idea of a theme for your life. If none come to mind, look up key words in a concordance and see what emerges. You may find a biblical character with whom you connect, such as Martha or Barnabas. Or perhaps your theme Scripture will be a familiar verse. Following are some common choices:

- "I can do all things through [Christ] who strengthens me" (Philippians 4:13, NRSV).
- "Nothing in all creation can separate us from God's love for us in Christ Jesus our Lord!" (Romans 8:39, CEV).
- "Be strong and bold; have no fear or dread of them, because it is the LORD your God who goes with you; he will not fail you or forsake you" (Deuteronomy 31:6, NRSV).
- "Trust in the LORD forever, for in the LORD GOD you have an everlasting rock" (Isaiah 26:4, NRSV).

After you select a verse, personalize it as needed. A personalized version of Romans 8:39 might read as follows: "Nothing in all creation can separate me from God's love for me in Christ Jesus my Lord." You may find yourself deciding on a theme Scripture based on its appropriateness for your life right now. In that case, as your situation changes, your theme Scripture is likely to change as well.

Processing this step can be helpful and enjoyable for both small groups and individuals. In chapter 8 we will look at how a church body can determine its theme Scripture.

● ● ● ● ● ● ● ● ● ● ● ● ● ● ● ●

INGRID'S STORY

"Those who wait for the LORD shall renew their strength, they shall mount up with wings like eagles, they shall run and not be weary, they shall walk and not faint" (Isaiah 40:31, NRSV).

As a child, I watched eagles and other large birds swoop gracefully through the air, and I wished I could fly too. As a young adult, I tried running but soon gave it up for energetic walking.

While Isaiah's words originally comforted God's people who languished in captivity in Babylon, they give me assurance too. I know I will never literally soar like an eagle or run long distances. Walking is my daily regimen, even now as a senior adult. Yet inside I can soar with the grace of an eagle. As I wait on God, expecting divine guidance, I develop a heightened spiritual endurance. Because God revives and renews me, I can flourish.

● ● ● ● ● ● ● ● ● ● ● ● ● ● ● ● ●

SUSAN'S STORY

"Do not be conformed to this world, but be transformed by the renewing of your minds, so that you may discern what is the will of God—what is good and acceptable and perfect" (Romans 12:2, NRSV).

This verse reminds me that at any time in life we can be transformed. Life is a growing experience! Scientific studies show that the human brain can be renewed by learning. Mental stimulation enables the brain to rewire itself.[2]

My mother had one year of college; my father had only a high school education, but both of them were stellar examples of lifelong learning. They were curious and open. Influenced by them, each graduation for me (high school, college, graduate school, retirement) became a new beginning rather than an ending. Living by this verse makes life an adventure of constantly learning and growing while seeking to discern God's will.

● ● ● ● ● ● ● ● ● ● ● ● ● ● ● ● ●

Find or Establish a Faith-Connection Group

Participating in a group in which you can study and grow is an essential part of spiritual health. The group might be a Bible study group, a Sunday church school class, an outreach ministry group, a gender-specific group, a special interest group, or an accountability group. If you can't find a group to suit your needs within your church, talk with your pastor about starting a new one.

Some people are reluctant to join a group, but when they do, they find that the group enriches their lives. If the thought of being part of a "permanent" group is daunting for you, explore the possibilities of a limited-term study or outreach activity at your church.

A small group offers a safe haven for people to be themselves. Minimal commitments by members usually include regular attendance, participation, and the practice of confidentiality. Facilitators work to foster a nonthreatening atmosphere where participants can build caring relationships. Small groups are communities where our God-given value is recognized, appreciated, and allowed to blossom.

One such community thrives in a small town in the Blue Ridge Mountains. When Tom and Eileen retired from pastoral ministry, they decided to form a Bible study group comprised of people with no meaningful relationship to Christ or a church. During their first year of retirement, they settled into their new home, became acquainted with their neighbors, and served as volunteers at the local soup kitchen. As they built relationships, they prayed for discernment on whom to invite to their group.

An astonishing group of people eventually signed on. Included were a Fortune 500 CEO, a dentist, a college teacher, a landscape designer, a computer specialist, a banker, a surveyor, a real estate agent, a contractor, some nurses, and some homemakers. Tom and Eileen agreed that the Bible would stand on its own. They didn't try to convince anyone of its truth, nor did they overtly function as evangelists. Instead, they believed that the Holy Spirit would call forth whatever good might emerge among group members.

Tom asserts that facilitating this group has been one of the most rewarding experiences of his entire ministry. Discussions have been lively and stimulating. As facilitators, Tom and Eileen have witnessed dramatic attitudinal changes. Group members have moved away from caution, skepticism, and cynicism to opening themselves to whatever God might have in store for them. Along the way, Tom and Eileen have had significant personal conversations with individual participants about what it means to respond in faith to God. But both of them know that it is difficult to take this step when one has intellectual issues or no previous exposure to the gospel, or has been dechurched. They remain faithful, providing a place for people to connect.

Explore What You Can Do to Strengthen Your Faith Community

For some people, the process of discovering what they can do to strengthen their faith communities is easy. For others, it takes time and careful thought. Begin by listing a number of things you could do to strengthen your church. It may mean becoming actively engaged in an existing outreach program of the church, working to begin a new one, becoming involved in teaching, or any number of other possibilities. As you work through the process, you may find that what you think of first is not possible. List the pros and cons for each of your options to help you make a decision.

At age eighty, Edith could have backed away from any new responsibilities at church. But she learned that in her inner-city neighborhood, the homeless had no place to find a hot meal on Mondays. She decided her church could provide one. Other people in the church thought the idea was noble but simply not possible. The size of the congregation had dwindled, and available human and financial resources were just not sufficient. Nevertheless, Edith went to the missions committee every time they met and pled her case. Finally, the committee agreed to experiment with a Monday lunch for ten weeks. However, the condition the committee set was that Edith would have to organize every bit of it. (Some members of the committee admittedly figured that would be the end of this crazy idea.)

Edith became a force to be reckoned with! She drafted the seniors in the congregation to prepare and serve the lunches. She cornered employed members of the congregation after church on Sunday. When they responded that they couldn't possibly help because of their jobs, she immediately asked them to contribute financially. And everyone did.

After ten weeks, it was evident that the Monday lunches were successfully serving a need in the community, and the mission committee was bragging about its new outreach program. This ministry fed the hungry for years. Edith strengthened her faith community.

Seek Balance

Make a four-column chart and label the columns FAMILY, WORK, CHURCH, and ME. In each column, list all the tasks you can think of in which you are currently engaged. Under FAMILY you might list things like taking out the trash, changing the oil in the car, paying bills, etc. In the ME column, you may list physical exercise, meditation, or anything you do to take care of yourself. Review the list. As you move through life, certain columns will take priority at various times. For example, if you have a newborn child in the home, the workload changes. At any given time, one column will be longer than the others. That is understandable. Next, look carefully to see if the listings in some columns are simply insufficient. Or examine the long columns to determine whether some listings could be released, at least for a time.

Family	Work	Church	Me

As one group did this exercise, they added a fifth column labeled INCIDENTALS. In this column they listed activities such as watching television, playing computer games, engaging in pointless phone conversations, or texting. If the television viewing was part of a planned family night, it went in the FAMILY column; otherwise it went to INCIDENTALS. They called these things "mindless time eaters." Reducing the number of mindless time eaters makes it easier to rebalance the rest of the time.

Now make a similar chart, and in each column write your primary hope for that category of your life. This should be done in the light of your theme Scripture.

This exercise helps put things in perspective. It does not resolve some of the areas of heavy workload and other demands on your time, but it often reveals some things that can be handled more efficiently and with more grace and joy.

Honor Your Work

God honors work. "The LORD God took the man and put him in the garden of Eden to till it and keep it" (Genesis 2:15, NRSV). One of the Ten Commandments is "Six days you shall work, but on the seventh day you shall rest" (Exodus 34:21, NRSV). Even in his pessimistic approach to life, the writer of Ecclesiastes found something good to say about work: "There is nothing better for mortals than to eat and drink, and find enjoyment in their toil" (Ecclesiastes 2:24, NRSV). Be assured that wherever we work—in the marketplace, at home, on the assembly line, or in a high-rise office building—our work matters to God.

If God honors work and our work matters to God, we also should honor our work. Honoring our work doesn't mean being prideful or full of ourselves. It simply means accepting ourselves and what we do as being worthy of honor.

Do you disrespect the work you do? Check your language. Listen to hear whether you belittle yourself in your conversations.

Try to go through a day without saying anything negative about yourself. Try a day of not saying anything negative about your family. Then try a day of not saying anything negative about your church. If a day is easy, try a week. There are, of course, times when we must do some self-examination, times when we must guide and discipline children, and times when we must speak honestly if called on to formally evaluate an employee. But beyond that, getting rid of 95 percent of the negative talk that comes out of our mouths may well be transformational.

While the Bible cautions us not to think more highly of ourselves than we ought to think (Romans 12:3), it does not tell us to think *less* of ourselves than we ought to think. Another way to honor your work is to celebrate your achievements. And don't wait for the really big ones to come along. Celebrate small victories. Recognize milestones. It is okay to give yourself kudos. Invite those you love to celebrate with you.

Study and Practice Spiritual Disciplines

Another critical step toward spiritual health is the practice of spiritual disciplines. These are habits or practices that help open us to God. Often people find a list of classical disciplines, such as those proffered by Richard Foster in his book *Celebration of Discipline*, to be an impossible package. Busy with careers and families, they ask, "Who has the time to explore the deeper realms of spirituality?" In their rush through daily life, they relegate spiritual disciplines to the contemplatives and clergy.

When pastors are able to demonstrate a personal life practice of the disciplines, it becomes easier for laity to begin to understand and try out specific disciplines. In the same way, there are laity who inspire clergy with their spiritual practice.

Richard Foster lists the internal disciplines as meditation, prayer, fasting, and study. He lists the external disciplines as simplicity, stewardship, solitude, submission, service, and evangelism. The corporate disciplines he suggests are confession, worship, guidance, and celebration.[3]

Sometimes alternative words are more engaging. Some Christians are nervous about the word *meditation*. If that word is a stumbling block, switch to "devotional time." A preliminary step to "fasting" is "balance and reason" in eating. Rephrase as needed.

Teaching and further definition is needed to understand each of the disciplines. For example, solitude may seem like sweet escape to the mother of four but scary and hollow to the disabled widower. It is important to know that solitude is more than a vacation and is not the same as loneliness. Consider some of the other disciplines. Stewardship is not only about giving money to the church; rather, it applies to the whole of life. Submission, as Foster suggests, is an act of humility, not the endurance of abuse. Simplicity may seem too challenging for our complex lifestyles, but we can move toward that discipline by taking single, more manageable steps.

There is nothing magical about the disciplines. They are merely tools to aid in our spiritual formation, tools that chip away at the exterior, eventually unveiling our God-given identity.

The Imperative for Wholeness

Taking the above seven steps seriously is important for church leaders, because spiritually unhealthy leaders endanger the congregation. Eli, an energetic young preacher, came to a healthy church. His knowledge of the Bible was contained in rote answers. He believed he had the scriptural answer to every life question and could quote it quickly. He used his Bible as a weapon.

The church had operated with democratic governance for more than a hundred years. However, in his eighteen months as pastor, Eli had established an all-male elder board whose members served for life. He also decided who was holy enough to serve in this capacity. Again, thinking he was following Scripture, he decided that members needed to publicly confess their sinful practices and attitudes. The church was on its way to chaos.

The women in the congregation suddenly found themselves on the sidelines. Likewise, the men who were not dubbed "holy" enough soon felt the effects of the unhealthy hierarchy. So instead of creating an environment for growth, the pastor had created an unhealthy atmosphere of distrust, animosity, and apathy. Instead of increasing the leadership base, he forced qualified and willing leaders to disengage. The stage was set for failure.

But the pastor wanted desperately to succeed. He came believing that his governance model and approach to ministry would make this healthy congregation even stronger. He didn't take time to get to know the people and develop a profound love for them. Neither did he listen to the people he served nor understand the nature of humility. His own personal practice of spiritual disciplines was sloppy and, at times, nonexistent. Sadly, Eli was unaware of his need for a healthy spiritual guide. When he left this church, he carried his frustration with him, endangering yet another congregation.

Spiritually healthy laity and clergy can work together to enhance God's kingdom. Alex and Marie had just graduated from seminary when they accepted the call to serve a church in a small town. Their theological training gave them plenty of ideas that they were eager to put into practice. The church welcomed their leadership, and the first two years were filled with learning experiences for both the pastors and people. But then the honeymoon ended.

The clergy couple had come from a metropolitan area to a community setting that they began to find stifling. Everybody in town knew who they were but kept them at a distance because they hadn't yet lived there for thirty years. Some of their discomfort in the community spilled over into the life of the church. Negativism raised its ugly head. However, the leaders of the congregation were not content to let negativism breed more negativity.

Since the congregation cared deeply for their pastors, they formed a faith-connection group. The group consisted of the pastors and several leaders from their own congregation as well as from a sister church in a neighboring town. Together they discussed the faith value of the work in which each was involved. The process they used helped the pastors to see that what they were doing in this small community was making a difference in people's lives. The dialogue also uncovered ministries for which the laity could provide leadership. Everyone experienced growth. Some learned and began practicing new spiritual disciplines. Most found additional ways to bring balance to their lives. Positive self-talk spilled over into the lives of both churches.

After several years, Alex and Marie accepted a call from a church in a medium-sized city. They look back at the years they spent at their first church with appreciation. They remain grateful for the lessons they learned, many of which they have been able to implement in their new setting.

QUESTIONS for Personal Reflection or Group Discussion

1. Think of people you know whom you perceive to be spiritually healthy persons—people who live their faith both inside and outside of the church. What might you learn from them?
2. How have you experienced the interconnectedness of spiritual, mental, and physical health? For example, do you often catch a cold when you are under additional stress? Has a sense of God's presence in your life given you energy you thought you didn't have? Has your anger at a person or situation ever made it hard for you to connect with God in prayer?
3. What tactics might you employ to keep a healthy motivational perspective regarding your work?

4. How can you approach wholeness and balance when you are overwhelmed by crises?
5. Since the journey toward wholeness is a lifelong process, what resources do you need to maintain the course?

Notes

1. *The Gospel of Thomas*, Saying 70, trans. Thomas O. Lambdin, http://www.sacred-texts.com/chr/thomas.htm (accessed January 13, 2011).

2. "The Human Brain," The Franklin Institute, http://www.fi.edu/learn/brain/exercise.html (accessed February 8, 2011).

3. Richard J. Foster, *Celebration of Discipline* (New York: HarperCollins, 1988), table of contents.

CHAPTER 7

Burden-Lifted Leadership

When more church members discover what it truly means to be disciples in the world, we will have enough leaders in the church. The key is in the wholeness. When faith permeates all of life, we live in a state of Immanuel—God with us. Church becomes a joyous refueling station—a place of encouragement, hope, joyous conviction, and celebration. A place where people are reenergized for moving mountains; changing systems; ministering to the least, the lonely, and the locked out. A place where each person is seen, heard, respected, and loved. Who wouldn't want to take a turn at "burden-lifted" leadership?

To be that refueling station, a healthy church will continuously emphasize a sense of wholeness for the congregation. Here are seven steps that can help a church move toward wholeness:

1. Define your church.
2. Structure for responsiveness.
3. Engage intergenerationally.
4. Offer meaningful worship opportunities.
5. Practice genuine affirmation and encouragement.
6. Establish a learning community.
7. Engage in community action.

Define Your Church

To define your church, begin with the "Find Your Church in the Bible" exercise described on pages 111–112. Include everyone in the process by engaging Sunday church school classes and other small groups. Then initiate a process to work toward the adoption of vision and mission statements. (See additional suggestions in chapter 8.)

In the "missional" church, the congregation sees itself focused outward instead of inward. That doesn't mean the inside isn't important. It means the inside is a place of renewing encouragement and energy that propels the congregation outward in caring service. When the congregants see what happens inside the church as being essential to its outreach, they find that the work of the church makes more sense.

Churches are not clubs, social service agencies, or arts groups. These other organizations are valuable assets to any community, but they are not faith communities. We join clubs to focus on a particular activity, such as square dancing, quilting, or public speaking. We participate in service groups to address a particular need, such as building homes for the homeless or promoting community fitness. We support arts groups knowing that vigorous arts programs improve quality of life.

The church is similar to a club in that it is a place of fellowship and belonging. It is similar to a service agency in that it responds to people in need. It is similar to an arts organization in that it promotes quality music in particular and, to varying degrees, other arts as well. What is different about a church is that at its best, it is part of the transcendent. It is connected from everlasting to everlasting. We focus outward toward the needs of our communities and the world because of God's love that dwells deep within us.

In all we do, we are sustained by the God of the universe. A classic hymn from the 1800s, often rewritten over the years, describes the connection like this: "Since Christ is Lord of heaven and earth, / How can I keep from singing?"[1] For us, the singing is serving. It is a deeply joy-filled response to God's magnificent love.

Leaders in the church will vary in the way this spiritual connectedness is made manifest. But each of us needs to know the presence of God in our lives.

Oak Street Church

Oak Street Church used to be a traditional church with the usual Sunday church school, worship, Wednesday night family supper and prayer meeting, weddings, funerals, and so on. Membership was fairly steady with just the slightest decline. The congregation didn't really experience any peak moments, but then there weren't any real valleys either. The church had no impact on the community in which it was located. It was just "there."

One Sunday a denominational leader who was unknown to this congregation visited the church. As she entered the sanctuary, she was greeted warmly by a man waiting by the door. As they talked, he asked, "What brought you here this morning?" When she told him who she was, he seemed a bit dejected by her answer. "Oh, I've been praying and praying that someone who needed the gospel would come through the doors this morning. But you don't need it." Her response was that it was always good to receive the gospel. Later she related the story and observed, "I couldn't help but wonder if he would just wait inside the building forever."

The pastor, whom we'll call John Smith, decided to accept his denomination's invitation for the church to participate in a renewal process with a group of churches. The process was called "Good Soil." Reverend Smith didn't have a really strong feeling about it, but he felt the congregation should do something with other churches from time to time. The church council didn't have a problem with it. What happened surprised them all, and the church was never the same. (More information on "Good Soil" can be found on pages 113–116.)

Through this process, Oak Street Church began to realize that its primary ministry was in the world outside the walls of the church. This realization transformed the church. The congregants now spend less time fussing with internal housekeeping items, such as what color the paint in the fellowship room should be and whether it is an insult to God to use permanent flower arrangements rather than fresh flowers on the altar. The emphasis now is on seeking to be the body of Christ, reaching out with a variety of community ministries. The church participates in feeding programs, counseling, and prisoner assistance. Because the church building is right across from a downtown park, the congregants are also sponsoring special events in the park. The Easter egg hunts and music concerts draw many more people than would have walked into the church.

In addition, younger members are now taking more leadership roles. One of these younger leaders indicated that he enjoyed participating because the church was doing things that were making a difference. He is finding in the church the authenticity that people are seeking.

Mapleview Church

Mapleview is a church in an urban neighborhood. A few years ago, the church realized a need to offer a food pantry to needy people in the area. Once a month, the pantry doors are open and people are able to stock up on things they need. The pastor was asked what kind of impact the food pantry had on the church's sense of identity, and he responded, "Tremendous!" He said it provides the opportunity for hands-on mission. The church had always seen itself as being mission-minded, but now, in addition to engaging in missions across the country and around the world, this church has found the mission on its doorstep. Its understanding of its identity as a church is made manifest in this service.

Some in the congregation have raised questions about the space the food pantry requires, and others have questioned whether all the people who come to the pantry are truly needy. Zeal for mission can be dampened when confronted with right-on-our-doorstep realities. The pastor's perspective is that dealing with local mission expands understanding of all mission, and in the case of this church, it has been significantly more positive in the life of the congregation than negative. (The Mapleview story continues later in this chapter.)

Faith Church

In a small, dusty western town, a little, white frame church called Faith Church had very few members. The people in the church and its denominational family all expected it to die before long. But two women decided to pray and to pray vigorously. They got the church involved. The congregation spent a year praying and seeking to find their church in Scripture. (See the "Find Your Church in the Bible" process described on pages 111–112.) Slowly things began to change. Church leaders found lost energy. People began to feel life rather than death when they came together. It didn't happen overnight, but it happened. They found a part-time pastor who discovered a congregation with limitless possibilities because of the spiritual renewal already at work. The church grew and flourished. The burden of serving became energizing ministry. Within a few years, the church was filled with people.

Now the pastor realizes that it is time to follow a similar process to turn the church outward. She says that the people have found so much joy in the rebirth of the church that their focus has become excessively inward. They have, in their happiness, forgotten the process that got them there. They are now returning to finding their church in Scripture and reaffirming their call to reach out.

Structure for Responsiveness

Restructuring simply for the purpose of restructuring or just because an author told you to do so will not be very satisfying. Look carefully at your mission statement. Engage members of the congregation in discussion about what steps would help you live into the mission. Then ask, "What kind of structure would help us to do this?"

In the first half of the twentieth century, churches seemed to grow by adding boards and committees. It was considered an honor to serve. In some churches, seeking the chairperson's role in a committee became highly competitive. Community leaders benefited from having church leader credentials. A successful local church leader typically went on to take an office in an association and region of the denomination. Everyone seemed to want a title. The way to hold newcomers was to get them onto a committee as soon as possible.

In the last half of the twentieth century, the overgrown structures became a problem as people sought more freedom. Serving on a board or committee began to feel more like a burden than an honor. Churches appeared to resemble bureaucratic systems instead of places of ministry. The image of the church as the body of Christ was very faint.

Mapleview Church, mentioned earlier, is a thriving church with more than three hundred members. It has two Sunday morning worship services in English and one in Sudanese. At one time, it had a structure of a church council and boards of deacons, trustees, Christian education, mission, and so forth. Nearly twenty years ago, the church invited in a consultant to guide them through a process that included a congregational survey and listening sessions. As a result, they restructured using a one-board system. This group is called the Spiritual Leadership Team. It has successfully guided the church ever since. Members are elected by the congregation as a whole and serve overlapping terms of office.

The current pastor came to the church following the restructuring and has found it fits well with the church's sense of itself. "I was attracted to this church," he said, "because it has the heart of a missional church…and had it before we even used the term *missional*." The focus of the church is on its ministry and mission to those in need outside the church building, both in the neighborhood and around the world.

Engage Intergenerationally

How often do we describe our local church as family? We know that being family, whether by kinship or faith, is not easy. In each generation, we struggle to accept and bridge our own versions of the generation gap. And unfortunately, each generation seems to believe the next generation is on a downward slide from its own. Older people tend to look at younger people with suspicion or concern. Younger people embrace newfangled technologies and strange ideas. And they dress differently or wear their hair in outrageous styles.

Of course, younger people pick up on these attitudes. They believe older people don't take them seriously. In many cases, younger people don't take older people seriously either. They think older adults are old-fashioned and just don't "get it." As a result, older people often feel unappreciated by younger people.

Surely it is fair to suggest that the source of many power struggles in our local churches may be found in tensions between generational age groups. It is no wonder then that older adults become anxious about promoting younger people to positions of authority and responsibility in the church. Likewise, why are we surprised that so many younger adults walk away from the church of their youth—and never return to the established church?

Mutual honor and respect are key to closing the generation gap. It is easier to find common ground on which to base honor and respect when we *know* people. Intergenerational programming can help connect the generations in your church.

Older adults want to remain productive and useful. They have a lifetime worth of skills that they can use to benefit the community. They are often looking for new friendships and learning opportunities. Older adults have valuable stories to tell the next generations.

Younger people also want to be recognized and valued. They want to contribute to society and make the world a better place. They have learned unique skills that they can teach others. They have exciting dreams and ideas to share. Often they are willing to listen to another person's story, or in the right environment can develop that willingness.

Together, young and old and those in between can increase their confidence and skills and forge new friendships. People in every generational group can fill the roles of learner and teacher as they collaborate to build a better community. Together they can practice mutual respect.

Typically, church activities are age-segregated. As a result, we learn only from those who are roughly our own age. However, for the church community to be whole, we need to have relationships that cross age boundaries. With intentionality and the right tools and leaders, the local church can be a vital intergenerational community. Young, old, and everyone in between will be the beneficiaries. What opportunities exist in your church for people to engage in projects together, listen to each other, and share with each other across generational lines?

Offer Meaningful Worship Opportunities

Meaningful worship is central to healthy congregational life. For many people, the weekly worship experience is their only regular link to the church body. While worship is prominent in the life of the church, it is also a source of conflict and confusion in many congregations.

How shall we worship? How can our services simultaneously attract seekers and satisfy traditional members? How can we communicate our faith to another generation when we express our worship in such different ways? Should we change our worship style to accommodate the expectation of various groups?

Jesus' words to the Samaritan woman at the well are clear: "God is spirit, and those who worship [God] must worship in spirit and truth" (John 4:24, NRSV). Worship is not simply about getting together to sing songs and listen to someone speak. Worship is about God. We honor God with our worship when we allow God's Spirit to break through the walls that separate us from our brothers and sisters. Our worship honors God when we strip ourselves of our prejudices and enter into fellowship with other members of the body of Christ. When we do, we find ourselves ministering to God in praise and thanksgiving, and God in turn ministers to us.

After all, worship is up to the worshippers. Worship is the act of expressing awe and devotion to God. What goes on between us and God is critical to the experience of worship. In order for true worship to take place, our minds need to be free from distractions and our hearts full of adoration. So what do we do to prepare for worship?

Perhaps we begin our preparation on Saturday night. A Native American tradition calls for preparation to begin at dawn on Sunday. Maybe we don't get up any earlier than we absolutely have to on Sunday morning. Regardless, the hour or so before church can be a difficult time. Distractions seem to persist; challenges usually arise. Just being aware of the possible barriers will help us enter the corporate worship experience with a spirit of expectancy. When we take the initiative to be spiritually primed for worship and assume responsibility for the outcome, we meet God and the experience is an enriching one.

Just as personal preparation for worship is vital, so too is preparation by the pastor(s), worship leader(s), and musician(s).

Worship is most effective when planned as a cohesive whole. Even the most seemingly informal style is best when carefully planned. One pastor reported that when she arrived to serve a small church, she discovered the organist routinely picked all the hymns for worship—and did so once a year. This was not a church that followed the lectionary; the organist simply picked hymns she liked and scheduled them a year in advance with no regard to the topic of the sermon or the situation of the congregation. This may be an extreme example, but it is worth noting.

Worship planning carried out by a small creative group of two or three along with pastoral staff is usually most effective. As they begin, they reflect on the theme Scripture or topic and then identify the worship elements that will best communicate the central idea. Based on the needs, they then involve people who are spiritually gifted to provide the desired leadership. In addition to the regular worship elements, they may consider including storytelling, drama, liturgical dance, art, and other creative expressions that engage multiple senses. As laity and clergy work side by side to integrate the elements of worship into a seamless whole, they prepare a strong foundation for meaningful worship.

Practice Genuine Affirmation and Encouragement

"The joy of the LORD is your strength" (Nehemiah 8:10, NRSV). A churchwide habit of affirmation and encouragement strengthens leadership. In chapter 5 we looked at the power of affirmation in raising up new leaders, particularly children and youth. But the practice can and should include the entire congregation. This is a critical step in moving toward church wholeness.

Affirmation and encouragement require a positive outlook. This positive outlook makes it possible to accomplish more than can be imagined.

Following the emancipation of slaves after the Civil War, missionary Joanna P. Moore left DeKalb, Illinois, and traveled to an island in the Mississippi to assist newly freed people. The situation in which she found herself was like a refugee camp. She became intensely focused on what would help immediate needs and then what would change the future outlook for the people. One of her many accomplishments was to establish Fireside Schools, home-based schools for women and children. She was judged harshly by some but remained determined. She continued to serve in African American communities until the end of her life at age eighty-three in 1916.

What would keep a person working through all these years? A key can be found in a message she sent to her supporters:

> I still keep tight hold of the Bible. My New Year's message for 1902 is "Now the God of hope fill you with all joy and peace in believing, that ye may abound in hope through the power of the Holy Spirit" (Rom. 15:13). Oh, beloved friends, be hopeful, be courageous. God cannot use discouraged people. The above text tells us we get our hopefulness by faith and in the power of the Holy Spirit. Free for all. Take and rejoice.[2]

Healthy Christians and healthy churches engage in the practice of joy. Joy is deeper than happiness. Joy is a sustaining power that results from being assured of God's presence and love. It is a partner with hope. Effective leaders share joy, and the expression of deep and abiding joy attracts and energizes members and leaders.

In John 15, Jesus called himself the Vine and said that we are the branches. Connected to the Vine, we elect to follow Christ's commandments and abide in his love. In verse 11 he said, "I have said these things to you so that my joy may be in you, and that your joy may be complete" (NRSV). In Jesus' prayer for his followers recorded in John 17:13, he prayed "I speak these things in the world so that they may have my joy made complete in themselves" (NRSV).

The practice of affirmation and encouragement is powered through recognizing the joy of the Lord as our strength and sharing that joy with others.

Establish a Learning Community

Romans 12:2 calls us to be transformed by the renewing of our minds. That is good stewardship of the mental capacity God gave us to become lifelong learners. When people stop learning, they stop growing. Some of us may be scholars; most of us are ordinary people seeking to follow Jesus. All of us can be stewards of our minds.

David Laubach, in his book *12 Steps to Congregational Transformation*, acknowledges that church leaders are, like all of us, ordinary people.

> Jesus' job description to be one of his followers demands everything, and Jesus takes on a group who apparently did not count on Calvary. Jesus will likewise teach and coach us through Scripture and stretch us when our plans are different from his plans. Jesus did not replace any of his fallible first followers. He worked with this unlikely group he believed could be the foundation of Christendom and gave them the leadership gifts, experiences, and Holy Spirit they would need to continue his work.[3]

Healthy churches provide ways for members and friends to engage in a lifelong journey of learning and growing. In northern parts of the United States, winter can seem interminable. A number of communities have developed a way to find fresh ideas, stimulate thinking, and enjoy a renewed sense of community in the deepest part of winter. They practice a partnership of community and university to promote lifelong learning on a variety of topics. Classes are offered every Sunday afternoon and evening throughout January. Churches, businesses, civic groups, and the local college or university have found enthusiastic response to the special winter courses. Classes involve an interesting mix of people in vigorous discussion on an extremely wide variety of topics. One year the topics in a particular community included The Holy Land, Quilting, Minor Prophets, Appreciating Wine, The Changing Nature of Church Music, Corn Genetics, and a history of the local county. Some of the most popular classes address issues of faith connecting with or conflicting with the secular issues of the day.

One of the outcomes of these special January experiences is the friendships that have developed among members of different churches, university students, staff and faculty, and others not connected with either. A few churches have follow-up studies with their own congregation following the January classes. These follow-ups provide an opportunity for the members of a congregation to reflect on what they have learned and how they feel about what people with very different beliefs shared in the classes.

What about churches that do not encourage and celebrate lifelong learning? Their congregants may struggle to hold tight to what they learned about their faith as children in Sunday school. They seem fearful of any new insights or perspectives. They want their church to remain restricted to a small body of knowledge. While the Bible warns us to be careful of the teaching of deceitful people, the Bible is very clear about renewing our minds. We are called to grow in the Spirit.

Lifelong learning is about growth. It helps us remain open to what God wants to teach us. It is cause for celebration.

Engage in Community Action

Eric Swanson and Rick Rusaw have written several books about the church that is turned outward rather than inward. "Becoming an externally focused church is not about becoming the best church in the community. The externally focused church asks, 'How can we be the best church for our community?' That one little preposition changes everything."[4]

We considered Mapleview Church earlier, but it is with its food pantry ministry that Mapleview impacts its community most directly. The reason for having the pantry is to respond with the love of Christ to people in need. The entire church feels ownership of this outreach, and numerous blessings have resulted, including the camaraderie that has grown among the members who work at the pantry. Pastor Paul says, "It gives joy!" Furthermore, this project has fostered small groups that have the satisfaction of doing mission in the neighborhood. By saying yes to this ministry, the church has become the hands and feet of Jesus in the community.

Not every church is called to set up a feeding program. The nature of outreach is based on the needs in the specific community. That may mean feeding the hungry, clothing the naked, welcoming the stranger, visiting those in prison and those who are sick, or working for the righting of wrongs.

● ● ●

The Seven Steps toward Church Wholeness help congregations increase their fruit-bearing capacity. In the process, new leaders emerge and long-term leaders are reenergized. Trying to provide leadership in a church that is not particularly fruitful feels like carrying a heavy burden. Serving as a leader in a church that is a healthy, fruit-bearing fellowship is an experience of joy.

QUESTIONS for Personal Reflection or Group Discussion
1. What does it mean to live in a state of Immanuel—in an awareness of God with us?
2. How do you respond to missionary Joanna P. Moore's statement, "God cannot use discouraged people"? Why?

3. In what ways does your church encourage and celebrate lifelong learning?
4. Can you think of an older person whom you have encountered who is a great example of a lifelong learner? What was unique about this person?
5. How have you experienced burden-lifted leadership?
6. Describe ways the leaders in your church are encouraged and affirmed.
7. How can your church be the best church for your community?

Notes

1. "How Can I Keep from Singing?" words and music by Robert Lowry (1826–99), public domain.

2. Joanna P. Moore, *In Christ's Stead: Autobiographical Sketches* (Chicago: Women's Baptist Home Mission Society, 1902), http://docsouth.unc.edu/church/moore/ill18.html (accessed February 9, 2011).

3. David Laubach, *12 Steps to Congregational Transformation* (Valley Forge, PA: Judson Press, 2006), 72.

4. Eric Swanson and Rick Rusaw, *The Externally Focused Quest* (San Francisco: Jossey-Bass, 2010), 3.

CHAPTER 8

Practical Strategies for Engaging and Retaining Leaders

As you have read the previous chapters, you have come across practical suggestions and many real-life illustrations. If you have picked up a few good ideas to try out, we are pleased. But you may still be asking, "How can we engage more of the laity in the total ministry of our church?" Perhaps by now you suspect there is no magic formula. There is no one-size-fits-all workshop to present or process to follow. But there *are* ideas that work.

This final chapter is a collection of some of those good ideas. They fall into the following broad categories:

- Sharpening the church's mission
- Preaching and teaching to grow leaders
- Developing leaders
- Leading leaders
- Appreciating leaders

Sharpening the Church's Mission

During the last twenty years, there has been much conversation about the missional church. Countless books have been published calling on churches to reclaim a missionary spirit, reaching out from a church building instead of hiding inside. In other words, bigger buildings, larger budgets, increased staffing, and self-serving programs are no longer at the forefront. Instead, the congregants seek to live out the call to be a "sent people."

The challenge for missional churches is to find the leaders and followers to make it work. So far it seems that churches with an outward focus are attracting leaders. People are seeking churches with integrity—churches that are doing their best to live up to their values.

The best strategy for nurturing leaders is for a church to be true to its mission. This authenticity adds vitality to church life and carries a church through difficult times as well. Consider these ideas:

Find Your Church in the Bible[1]

This exercise of finding your church in the Bible helps a congregation tell the church's story and serves as a foundation for subsequent work on vision and mission statements. A beginning point of transformation is an honest assessment of the present state of your church. Spiritual transformations always begin with God working from where we are.

Someone has said that salvation is the intersection of one's own story and "The Story"—that is, God's Story. When one's story meets God's Story, salvation happens. And where do we find God's Story? The Bible tells it over and over with each character, story, or writing. If we look, study, and pray, we will begin to see our own story there as well. The Bible is filled with stories that align with our own experience and seem to have been waiting to show us what God has in store for us. The same is true for churches. Where does your church's story cross God's Story in the Bible?

Begin by looking for characters, stories, or writings in the Bible that sound a lot like the current story of your church. This search may turn up a collection of biblical characters and stories that reflect the various dimensions of your church's story. Or you may find one story that clearly mirrors your church's narrative.

Engage your congregation in this search process. Conduct Bible studies around some of the possible texts, or ask the pastor to preach on them. What clues does "The Story" give you about how God might want to work in a transforming way in the story of your church?

Have fun as you engage in this discovery process. Don't close off the search too quickly. Rather, accept the challenge to keep going deeper and deeper into your story.

Develop or Revisit Your Church's Mission and Vision Statements

Mission and vision statements are powerful motivational tools. Ideally, a mission statement explains the church's reason for being. A vision statement looks to the future by defining the church's intended destination. When you compare several churches' mission statements, you will likely discover similarities. Vision statements, on the other hand, express diverse approaches to kingdom work based on God's unique call. In some instances, these statements are combined into one longer expression of purpose and plan for the future.

Here's an example from Prairie Baptist Church in Shawnee Mission, Kansas:

> Our Mission: Prairie Baptist Church is a Christian community committed to transforming the world through: worship, service, and spiritual formation. Spiritual formation is the process of being shaped according to the image of Christ by the gracious working of the Holy Spirit for the sake of the world.

> Our Vision: (how we intend to live out our purpose in the future) Prairie Baptist Church seeks to be an open, caring, and intentional community engaged in spiritual practices

that enrich our journey and deepen our connection to God, to one another, and to the world.[2]

Carefully crafted statements are catalysts for action. Many resources are available to assist in the process of developing a mission statement and a vision statement. Many books and websites on the subject provide specific guidelines, even "rules," as to how this should be done. A congregation that has engaged in the exercise of finding their church in the Bible will be well prepared for the actual writing process.

If your church would like to engage in a process that will lead to the development of key statements, turn next to your regional judicatory office. Staff in your executive minister's or bishop's office will be able to provide suggestions and save a local committee the task of plowing through multiple resources. If you choose to go to the Internet, avoid resources that are rigid and suggest there is only one "right" way to get this job done.

Church planning specialists agree that it is helpful for a group to know why it exists and what the group wants to accomplish. For a congregation to come to agreement, it is critical to engage the whole family in the journey to clarify its mission and vision. Mission feeds the confidence of the congregation. Vision fuels momentum. Both evolve as the congregational community changes.

Prepare Good Soil[3]
Gardeners and farmers know that a critical element in the success of a crop is the quality of the soil. Using this image, Richard Sutton and others developed a plan that gives small churches strategies for renewal. Renewal is dependent on the moving of the Spirit. But, to recognize and respond to the Spirit, the congregation must be prepared and ready. Recall the Parable of the Sower (Luke 8:4-8) where Jesus spoke about sowing seeds in various types of soil. Soil that is prepared yields greater results.

"Good Soil" is a process intended to develop congregational readiness. The process itself has been used by different groups under a variety of names. "Good Soil" is designed for use by groups of churches, but the concept can be used by individual churches as well. The outline that follows gives the basic ideas which in turn may be tailored for a specific church or group of churches.

Five or six churches commit to work together for the renewal of all. Each church appoints a renewal team made up of the pastor and at least two or three key opinion leaders in the congregation. The team meets three times a year with teams from the other churches. The process is designed for two years, but some groups that have found the process successful have continued beyond that time frame. Each team is responsible for leading the process in its own church. In some cases, the team may provide training to one of the other churches.

The thrice yearly Good Soil gatherings of the renewal teams from the participating churches begin with worship. Each time worship is done in a different style, such as traditional, Taizé, contemporary, emergent, or blended. The final worship service is in the style the worship leader chooses. It is good if all the worship times are planned by one pastor from outside the participating churches. This should be someone who can provide quality worship in each of the styles.

At each gathering time is set aside for sharing key results in each church and for prayer. An outside resource person teaches the gathered group.

> GATHERING 1: Preparing the Soil. This session includes an introduction to the process and teaching on spiritual disciplines. Covenant prayer groups are formed. At each gathering, time is given for these groups to pray together.

GATHERING 2: Planning the Garden. Participants focus on biblical and theological study on transformation as well as receive training on finding their church in the Bible (see pages 111–112) and on building a mission statement.

GATHERING 3: Planting the Seed. Churches share their progress on developing or revising their mission statements. The teaching is a survey of transformation literature and instruction in crafting a vision statement.

GATHERING 4: Dealing with Weeds. Teams share progress on vision statements and receive instruction in conflict transformation.

GATHERING 5: Nurturing to Harvest. Participants receive training on mission and community outreach.

GATHERING 6: Celebrating the Harvest. As at each gathering, groups worship, meet in their covenant prayer groups, and share local church stories and progress. This session ends with celebration and evaluation.

Between each gathering, the teams have the responsibility to take back what they've learned to their local churches. Other tasks of the renewal teams include weekly meetings where they plan and pray. They share with each other how they are doing with the practice of the spiritual disciplines. The success of the process depends to a great extent on how well the teams teach their churches and lead them in the process. It is critically important that the team not become a private club from which the congregation feels excluded.

One group that used this process included a variation. Each local church team led workshops at one of the other churches. Between gatherings 2 and 3, one team held a workshop on spiritual disciplines. Between gatherings 3 and 4, another team held a workshop on vision statements. At the end of the process, teams were encouraged to lead one of their sister churches in celebrating renewal. These workshops proved to be extremely valuable, because the team had to become comfortable enough with the content to actually lead a workshop. The fact that each local church experienced leadership from a sister church tended to validate the process. All in all, Good Soil gatherings can be valuable experiences of learning, sharing, and celebrating.

Preaching and Teaching to Grow Leaders
Offer Bible-Based Character Studies

In the early church, apostles, prophets, evangelists, pastors, and teachers worked "to equip the saints for the work of ministry, for building up the body of Christ" (Ephesians 4:12, NRSV). Ministry belonged to the "saints," the *laos*, the people of God. So who were these ministers? Prepare sermons or study sessions based on some of these interesting people.

Barnabas (Acts 4:36; 11:22-24). Barnabas was known as the encourager. He came from a Jewish family in Cyprus. A wealthy landowner and member of the Jerusalem church, he took Saul (later named Paul) and John Mark under his wing. Barnabas was the door through which Paul was allowed entrance into the early church community.

Churches can be dramatically changed when the majority of the congregation accepts the idea that they can be encouragers. A basic rule for encouragers, as we mentioned in chapter 6, is to speak the truth. Gushy, overdone compliments are easily ignored. Encouragement must be sincere. There is something positive to say about everyone. Find words of encouragement that truly build up, not judge or diminish. (Information on how to begin a Barnabas Patrol is found later in this chapter under "Developing Leaders.")

Euodia and Syntyche (Philippians 4:2). Even in the best of worlds, human beings experience conflict. Euodia and Syntyche were probably deaconesses in the church at Philippi who were caught up in some sort of disagreement. Paul knew that it would be worth the effort to resolve the differences between them. Why did he bother mentioning them? Because they were worth mentioning! These were leaders at odds with one another whom he deemed too valuable to lose. Resolving whatever was going on would strengthen the community of faith.

One of the problems in our culture is our inability to disagree without being disagreeable. Learning how to transform conflict is a component of healthy church life. (Some suggestions for transforming conflict are listed later in this chapter under "Developing Leaders.")

Priscilla and Aquila (Acts 18:1-3; Romans 16:3-4). Priscilla and Aquila were tentmakers. Their lives interfaced with Paul with whom they forged a business relationship and a lifelong friendship. They mentored Apollos and helped lead congregations in Corinth, Rome, and Ephesus. Some of these groups met in their home. The Scripture never mentions one without the other.

Priscilla and Aquila, like many people in today's churches, were deeply committed, knowledgeable, encouraging supporters of God's work. They were a seemingly unstoppable husband-wife team, yet they posed no threat to Paul. Instead, he valued them as partners. Perhaps the key lay in their friendship.

Moses (Exodus 3:1-12). God commissioned a sheepherder to be Israel's leader—and he wasn't just any sheepherder, but one in self-imposed exile after murdering an Egyptian. Moses didn't seem a likely leader, and he didn't volunteer; he was drafted. He was taking care of his father-in-law's sheep when he arrived at Mount Horeb, the mountain of God. There God spoke with clarity.

Moses' call consisted of the initial commissioning, his objection, and subsequent divine reassurance. Moses was catapulted into leadership. He spent the next forty years in the desert humbly walking with God and masses of disgruntled followers.

When God calls us into leadership, God doesn't abandon us. Rather, God walks with us. Moses' faith in the invisible God equipped him for long-term leadership.

Anna (Luke 2:36-38). Anna and other prophets were revered for their spiritual wisdom that equipped them to proclaim God's word to the people. A widow for eighty-four years, Anna literally lived at the temple. There she served God by fasting and praying. Her prayers likely expressed her longing for the Messiah. When Mary and Joseph presented Jesus at the temple, Anna recognized him as the one who would redeem Israel.

In our search for new leaders, we sometimes forget to tap into the wisdom of the years. Our elders have experienced more than we have. It makes sense to seek their input.

Luke (Colossians 4:14). Luke was primarily a physician. In his "free time," he wrote one-fourth of the New Testament—the Gospel of Luke and the book of Acts. As Paul's associate, he also participated in evangelism (Philemon 24).

Many scholars agree that Luke was "broad in his sympathies, compassionate toward the poor and the outcasts of society, genuinely pious, self-effacing, radiantly joyful, charmingly urbane, and deeply loyal."[4] In addition, he was a detail person. His precise analytical approach made him a valuable addition to any team. With these assets, Luke can be lifted up as a role model.

Lydia (Acts 16:14-15). Lydia was a successful businesswoman who sold purple dye and cloth. She was the head of her household, so she was probably either a widow or unmarried. A Jewish proselyte, she is remembered as the first known Christian believer in the West. The first church in Europe met in her home. When she extended hospitality to Paul, Silas, and Luke, she set the bar for the Philippian church.

Lydia was a busy woman, but not too busy to answer God's call. We should not presume that high profile people are too busy or too successful to be involved in the leadership of the church. As a rule, busy people have the ability to prioritize and get things done.

The Disciples (Luke 9). In chapter 2 we highlighted Jesus' twelve recruits. What an unusual team he chose! They didn't seem to have the "right stuff" to carry forward the work of the kingdom. Along with their inexperience, they were competitive, self-centered, and insensitive. Yet Jesus delegated important work to them, not just token responsibilities. They made mistakes, but he kept working with them. Over time these rookies developed into servant leaders.

Failure is forgivable. It often serves as a base for character development. Failure is certainly not the litmus test for elimination. Jesus didn't look for a perfect leadership team; neither should we. Rather, we seek faithful people who have a potential to grow and blossom.

Establish a Study Group Based on Vocational Ministry

Form a Sunday church school class or other study group that revolves around vocations. The group should have a facilitator. However, the actual teachers will be invited guests from a variety of occupations and professions. Each guest may lead the class for one session, several sessions, perhaps a month, or even an entire quarter. Ask the guest leader to focus on the question, "How does my faith impact my work?" Here's how it worked in one church.

At Grace Church, the young adult Sunday church school class invited guests to lead their class, highlighting the theme "My Faith on the Job." One of the teachers was a physician in the congregation. His teaching had a profound and lasting impact on the students. He taught about the way his faith influenced him in his day-to-day practice and decision making. He also talked about the intersection of science and faith. The discussion was vigorous. During this time, the young adults in this particular church did not drift away from the church as so many do. They found that the integrity and discipline of the various teachers curbed the cynicism about the church that is so often present in their peers.

The impact of this experience went beyond the young adults. The physician later reflected that the preparation for the class helped him focus his thinking about how his faith informed the work he did. Through this teaching, he felt more connected to his church than ever before.

Sermon Ideas
The following sermon ideas offer suggestions for further study. A pastor may adapt them for a sermon series, or a study group might use them as starting points for discussion.

Title: Time to Plant
Text: Isaiah 28:23-29
Purpose: To encourage congregants to action as God's people.
Concept: Farmers don't continuously plow their fields to get them ready for planting. Once they have prepared the soil, they plant seeds. Sometimes people in churches spend a lifetime getting ready to be God's people but don't actually get around to doing what they are called to do.
Note: What does it mean to take one step forward in faith? We may not suddenly transform the world, but what does it mean for each of us to be faithful? God will take care of the rest.

Title: Leading with Less Than Enough
Text: Luke 21:1-4 (NEB)

Purpose: To motivate persons in the congregation to step forward in a new ministry.

Concept: When Jesus saw rich people putting gifts in the treasury followed by a poor widow who had less than enough but gave what she had anyway, Jesus said that this woman had given more than the others. He praised the woman with two coins as an example for the rest of us. When we are asked to serve, is our perception that we have less than enough education, or time, or energy, or know-how? What happens when we open ourselves up and give what we have? God is not interested in what we don't have. God wants to show us what we do have.

Note: Just before this passage, Jesus was talking to his disciples about the sanctimonious scribes. They talked a good line but in the meantime were devouring widows' houses. It may be that Jesus was weary of the pride of the rich—the people with "more than enough."

Title: Increase the Harvest of Your Righteousness
Text: 2 Corinthians 9:6-15
Purpose: To call forth leaders in the congregation.
Concept: While it is important to recognize that this text was written about money, read it again, thinking of the sharing of talents. Look particularly at verse 10, "He who supplies seed to the sower and bread for food will supply and multiply your seed for sowing and increase the harvest of your righteousness" (NRSV). Can we see the good work of a leader stepping forward to take responsibility and using his or her God-given gifts as a harvest of that leader's righteousness?
Note: In verse 13, Paul writes about obedience and generosity in the sharing of one's gifts.

Three-Sunday Series: "Powerful Hope from Habakkuk"
Sunday 1 Title: Write the Vision
Text: Habakkuk 2:1-3a
Purpose: To motivate listeners to live in a manner that reflects God.
Concept: "Write the vision; make it plain on tablets, so that a runner may read it" (v. 2, NRSV). Our culture today is in many ways like a runner. We don't stop and wait on the Lord. Here God told Habakkuk to write the vision in a clear manner. What does it mean for us to write the vision? One way is simply to live in a way that makes the vision clear. Our God is the way, the truth, the life.
Note: Consider these two supplemental texts: "Go now, write it before them on a tablet, and inscribe it in a book, so that it may be for the time to come as a witness forever" (Isaiah 30:8, NRSV) and "You are a letter of Christ…written not with ink but with the Spirit of the living God, not on tablets of stone but on tablets of human hearts" (2 Corinthians 3:3, NRSV).

Sunday 2 Title: Get Priorities in Order
Text: Habakkuk 2:18-20
Purpose: To persuade worshippers to reorder the priorities in their lives.
Concept: The text asks, "What use is an idol?" What are the idols that pull our attention today? For many, it is some kind of materialism. We worship the power of the dollar. Success is measured in salary, the square footage of our home, or how many cars we own. For others, the idol is the image of ourselves we have created. The response of Habakkuk to the idolizing of gold and silver is to stop and stand before the people and say, "The LORD is in his holy temple; let all the earth keep silence before him!" (v. 20, NRSV). It is a command to stop, recognize who the Lord is, and remember who we are in the Lord.
Note: When we get our priorities in order, we find a new way. Our trust is in God who wants to "put a new song in [your] mouth, a

song of praise to our God. Many will see and fear, and put their trust in the LORD" (Psalm 40:3, NRSV).

Sunday 3 Title: Through It All—Praise God!
Text: Habakkuk 3:17-19
Purpose: To energize a congregation that may think it can't grow or reach out, or to uplift a congregation that is experiencing sorrow.
Concept: This amazing passage is a powerful message to a congregation that is going through tough or disappointing times. It may be that key leaders have moved away or died. It may be that in spite of all efforts, the church is not growing. It may be that things just seem to be less than expected. Habakkuk said it is time to rejoice! Rejoice even if there is no visible fruit. It is time to "exult in the God of my salvation. God, the Lord, is my strength; he makes my feet like the feet of a deer, and makes me tread upon the heights" (vv. 18a-19, NRSV). Andraé Crouch's song "Through It All" augments this theme.
Note: End the three-Sunday sermon series by affirming, "We are God's people! We will not be defeated in doing good! We will renew our faithfulness!"

Developing Leaders

Establish a Barnabas Patrol

The Barnabas Patrol was an accidental happening at Trinity Church. A Sunday church school class of senior adults was studying Barnabas. As they talked about his gift of encouragement, they began to think of ways they might become encouragers. It was a quiet project. They didn't make any big announcements or formally start a new program. As a class, they simply decided to become the "Barnabas Patrol."

Each Sunday they spent a few minutes of class time reporting on their "Barnabas" experiences. Their goal was to keep their encouragement genuine and seamless so that it would never seem contrived or part of a "program." They encouraged the pastor, parents, children, teachers, and kitchen workers. They kept their eyes open for good things to compliment. They watched for weary workers and offered words of deep thanks.

According to the pastor, this quiet little project has had an enduring effect on the church. Others in the congregation have become encouragers. And the seniors are not seen as ones who say, "We've never done it that way before." Instead, they have become people who see the possibilities. Looking for good has had positive results throughout the church but especially on the strengthening of leaders and the development of new leaders.

The Education of Little Tree is a book about a little boy who was raised by his Cherokee grandmother. The child, Little Tree, says, "Gramma said...when you come on something that is good, first thing to do is share it with whoever you can find; that way, the good spreads out to where no telling it will go. Which is right."[5] That is what the Barnabas Patrol does.

Provide Encouragement Cards

Some churches include encouragement in their budget. They provide simple, brightly colored postcard-sized encouragement cards in the pew racks. Congregants are invited to use the cards to write encouraging notes to people in the congregation. The cards are placed in the offering plates at the appropriate time during the service. Ushers hand-deliver some of them; the rest are mailed by office staff. The bright cards are never overlooked in the incoming mail, and they are always received with gratitude.

In one church, the idea of encouragement took hold in a significant way as a group decided to pray regularly for denominational leaders. From time to time, persons on the state and national staff received postcards from that church with a personalized note from a member indicating that prayers were being offered on their behalf. The cards were sent to support staff as well as executive staff. One card to the office manager of a state office expressed the church's appreciation for all the detail work she handled and her graceful manner in handling telephone requests.

Whether the encouragement cards are sent locally or nationally, they represent the ethos of a church. They present a simple and touching witness that leaders are valued.

Portray Leadership Positions as Worthwhile Work

What constitutes worthwhile work? What makes people want to get involved in the activities of the church? Here are some positive answers people have given:

- Being involved is enjoyable for me.
- Being involved makes me feel connected to God.
- Being involved gives me the satisfaction of making a difference and doing good.
- Being involved helps me get better acquainted with a wide variety of people.
- Being involved is good for my business.

What makes people *not* want to get involved in the activities of the church? Why is it perceived not to be worthwhile? Here are some negative answers people have given:

- Being involved eats up time I'd rather spend elsewhere.
- Being involved means working with people who aren't all that perfect.
- Being involved means someone will pick at or judge the work I do.
- I'd rather let other people do it.
- The activities at the church are self-serving and don't reach out.

Like it or not, these are *real* answers from *real* people in *real* churches. As we seek to develop leaders, our challenge is to portray church leadership as worthwhile work. What services would the person be helping to provide? What might personal rewards be? What need(s) will the person be helping to fill? How would service in this position utilize his or her spiritual gifts?

Implement the Simple Circle

Not everyone in church is moderator material, but probably more people have gifts for this than the church initially suspects. Nearly everyone can find some opportunity for leadership. And even the most confident leaders are better if they try a stint at being a follower. The Simple Circle is a method of rotating leadership and followership. Moving from being a follower to being a leader and back again is a healthy way to build community.

The congregation is invited to try the Simple Circle system of leadership rotation for a period of three years. Current leaders are affirmed and encouraged to support the idea as a way to engage more members of the congregation. For some leaders, it provides a break or sabbatical time in which they can try something new.

Prepare a list of as many jobs as possible and distribute it to the members. Ask participants to write their name under every job they would consider trying for a year. Each person who is willing to serve in a job will be asked to take on the task for twelve months, with a possible extension of a second year. Assure members that people who have held the jobs before will share what they've learned during their tenure.

At the end of the first or second year, each member is asked to take on a different job. At the end of the three-year period, the process is evaluated. Churches usually customize the rotation depending on the size of the church and the number of jobs. The goal is to have participants try at least two jobs during the three-year period. One way to initiate this experiment is to have an all-church gathering somewhat like a fair. Invite people to walk around to different stations and hear people "pitch" a particular job they have held. (Try this; you'll like it!) At the end of the fair, members sign, in as many places as possible, the job list they've been given.

Follow this activity with a time of prayer. Acknowledge the fun of hearing people try to sell their jobs. Invite God to be in the fun and in the seriousness of the jobs as they relate to the ministry of the church. Ask God to open new doors so that people have opportunities to try things they've never tried before.

In the week following the fair, a group consisting of the pastor and two others—probably one person who has leadership experience in the church (but is very flexible) and one with less experience—prayerfully work together to make the job assignments. It is important to find a task for everyone who turned in a form. If there are persons who mark only one job, you may need to talk with them about the need to have them do a different job. When

---

Example: Joe has been chair of the building maintenance committee for eighteen years because he is good at what he does. Some in the church have no interest in the job. Others might be willing to take a turn but don't want to be compared with Joe. One or two people would really like the job but wouldn't consider doing anything that might hurt Joe's feelings. There is even one person who really wants the job but has absolutely no aptitude for it.

Problems: No one will ever develop the skills to do this job as long as Joe does it. Joe is not being affirmed for anything other than his skills in this area. If this is Joe's core identity, you can't just turn him out without doing damage.

Possibilities: What if Joe stepped aside for a limited period of time but was available as a consultant? At the same time, Joe would try a new role. Another area of ministry would benefit from Joe's expertise, and another leader would emerge.

---

the job assignments are presented, have a commissioning service for the persons who commit to their new tasks.

In establishing the Simple Circle style, it is important to recognize different personality types. Some people love routine and thrive on it. Other people like everything to be different every day. Most people are somewhere in between. Encourage participants to try something outside their comfort zone. Trying something quite different for a year or two can help us understand the various essential jobs in the church and what it takes to get those jobs done. What often happens is that people discover new areas of interest and even competence that they never considered before. Assure people that in the end they will be given the opportunity to indicate the kinds of jobs in which they feel they have the most to offer.

One church combined the Simple Circle idea with a traditional spiritual gifts inventory. They encouraged individuals to try jobs they hadn't done before but that fit their "giftedness."

Planning is critical. Some churches are able to keep the Simple Circle simple. Others turn it into a confusing ordeal. The hope is that a church would be stimulated by the concept of the Simple Circle and use it to encourage members to try new jobs within the congregation. Try to keep it from becoming a rigid "straitjacket" of how things must be done. Prepare and present the idea as an enjoyable exercise to freshen everyone's perspective and discover latent talents. Adapt the process, but be guided by love and care for all members of the congregation.

Leading Leaders

Forge Networks and Teams

Utilizing the team concept is a proven way for churches to develop leaders. While some jobs in the church are best handled by one person, many are ready-made for teams. Churches have traditionally been good examples of team leadership. In most Protestant churches, these groups are known as the church council, ministry leadership team, or board of elders. Composed of the leaders of various boards or committees within the church, the council can be an effective venue for leadership development. Unfortunately, many church councils are bogged down with old ways of doing business and do not reflect church vitality.

To improve the capacity of the council to develop leaders, consider the following:

■ *Simplify reporting.* A meeting that consists of one lengthy report being read to the group followed by another and yet another is tedious at best. Change the focus from control to empowerment. Have members describe what their subgroup has done to help fulfill the church's mission or vision statement.

■ *Engage in creative visioning processes.* A group visioning process will produce much more than the sum total of the individual participants. Hold an annual retreat during which church leaders use creative lenses to look to the future. What two or three things can you emphasize that will help the church live up to its mission?

■ *Keep the council integrated into congregational life.* It is important to realize that the council is not a club separate from the congregation. If the council becomes distant from the congregation, the whole body risks loss of life and energy. The attitude becomes, "Let the council do it." The goal, instead, is to have the congregation say with pride, "That's our leadership team!"

Form Mentor Relationships

Mentoring is a dynamic process used to nurture and grow leaders. In fact, mentoring is one facet of discipling. Here's how one congregation benefited from mentoring: Bill had been in charge of the Sunday church school off and on for more than ten years. The moderator talked with Bill about being a mentor for the next Sunday church school leader. Some gentle persuading was necessary to get Bill to consider it. The moderator helped Bill learn what it means to be a mentor. When Bill's biggest challenge came—the new person wanted to make some changes in the way things were done—Bill was ready to be a mentor rather than feeling threatened.

Mentoring relationships may be formal or informal but are nearly always intentional. Mentors are typically older than their mentees, but experience, not age, is the primary qualifier. Mentors tell their stories of both success and failure. They share their insights, observations, and analyses, and they introduce mentees to people they need to get to know. Mentees, in turn, are encouraged to ask specific questions, seriously consider the mentor's advice, and invite constructive criticism. In order for the relationship to be productive, mentors and mentees should display mutual respect.

Teach Conflict Transformation

Where there are humans, there will, at some time, be conflict. We are each blessed with our own minds, and we don't always think alike. Unfortunately, not nearly enough churches have taken the time to develop conflict transformation skills. Untransformed conflict has killed churches, split churches, and caused leaders to quit or burn out under the pressure.

For a time, the buzzwords in management circles were *conflict resolution* or *conflict management*. Then it was *conflict mediation*. All of these have been helpful and can be utilized by churches. Perhaps it is most helpful for churches to think of the process as *conflict transformation*. Congregations can learn to turn conflict into transforming growth and development. Learning how to live together in new ways requires training.

Learning how to cope with conflict can have a beneficial impact on families, churches, communities, and beyond—all the way to international situations. Even if only for leader retention, it is worth the time and energy for churches to commit to transforming the way they respond to conflict.

Provide Lifelong Learning Opportunities

Provide continuing education classes for church leaders and others in the congregation who are interested. These classes might be held for four Sunday evenings or two consecutive Saturday mornings. They should be offered on a regular basis. Some resources from the world of business can be helpful to church leaders. Contact your judicatory to determine what denominational resources are available. Online resources are also available, such as Workshops for Church Life and Leadership at www.abhms.org/resources/church_life_leadership/.

The nominating committee at Good Shepherd Church was finding long-term leaders less interested in serving and potential leaders very hard to recruit. At one meeting of the committee, members began to talk about what was missing. Why did people like the church but resist leadership? The committee developed an unusual idea that was worth a try. They designed a promotional campaign touting the benefits of being a leader and promising to offer valuable training to those who would agree to serve. They crafted posters for the church building, bulletin inserts, and promo pieces for the website.

Pastor Margaret reported that not all the ideas were worth sharing with other churches, but the experiment did yield some positive results. She felt the most effective part of the promotion combined an appeal to serve God with the side benefit of gaining skills and experience transferable to other parts of life, on the job and at home. The committee marketed the two- or three-week leadership training sessions as incentives to taking leadership responsibilities. They shared what similar leadership seminars would cost in the secular world and offered job holders in their church the same content at no cost. The pastor felt that the creativity these ideas generated in the nominating committee sparked fresh approaches from other committees as well.

Reengage the Newly Retired

At the present time, the largest pool of potential volunteers in America consists of the newly retired. Large numbers of people who are retiring in their sixties remain in good health. Many of these are actively seeking meaningful ways to invest their time. Does the church represent to them a positive, challenging, meaningful, and enjoyable place to give their time? Or does the church represent for them tired, even tedious, routine? Is the church a place where they feel encouraged and affirmed? Or is it a place where they feel judged? Needless to say, the answers to these questions make a big difference for the individuals and for the church.

In chapter 5 we noted that there is no "retirement" from one's call to discipleship. It has been said that God's retirement system begins at death. Yet the ways in which a person carries out discipleship will change as life and health circumstances change. "Third stagers"—those who are in the third stage of life (stage 1 being one's growing-up years, stage 2 being career years, stage 3 being the rest of one's life)—are a valuable asset in any church. Disregarding the potential of this group is a sad mistake.

Mrs. Oglethorne has arranged the flowers for the sanctuary for thirty years. If someone suggests she try something else, she will probably have one of the following responses:

- Hurt—"Oh no, they want to take away my joy."
- Delight—"Finally! I am really tired of flowers."
- Surprise—"I thought I was only good enough to do the flowers."
- Self-pity—There's nothing else I know how to do."

The relationship between Mrs. Oglethorne and the church could be easily damaged by assuming her response. If the church has a group for third stagers, that group can explore what it means to trade in long-held jobs for new kinds of involvement.

Tap the Gifts of Homebound Leaders

People who must remain at home because of physical limitations have often been seen by the church as recipients of ministry rather than as active disciples. The healthy church engages these people in ministry that fits their life situations. Coordinating this ministry is a special leadership opportunity and can often be handled by a homebound person. Following are some ways to engage homebound leaders:

As prayer partners. Have a volunteer take a card with about four prayer concerns to homebound persons. Ask if they would be willing to be a prayer partner. Give them the card and ask them to pray daily for the next week on these particular concerns. Find out if they would prefer to get weekly updates by mail, phone, or e-mail. (Do not give them a long list of names and then have no further contact for six months.) Give someone on the church governing board the responsibility to phone or send a note every few months thanking them for their prayer ministry. From time to time on Sunday mornings, as the pastor asks the congregation to pray, the pastor should remind the congregation of the ongoing prayer ministry of the prayer partners.

As letter writers. Letter writing is nearly a lost art. Yet there is something special about taking mail out of the mailbox and discovering a real letter from someone. Some homebound persons are capable of and interested in a ministry of correspondence. They might start by writing notes to students away at college or to those in missionary or military service. If any member or relative of a member is incarcerated, writing to them can be an especially powerful ministry—not to preach at them, but simply to let them know there are people who care for them.

As phone chain members. To be successful, any phone chain needs periodic evaluation, including participant feedback. Phone chains exist in three basic forms:

1. A prayer chain is the most common type of phone chain. People pass along the congregation's prayer concerns. These chains are especially active during emergencies. Some work well and some fall into the category of gossip as members talk with one another under the cover of sharing prayer concerns.

2. Another type of phone chain is one to share congregational information or provide reminders of important events.

3. A third phone chain is one in which members of the congregation can check on homebound persons and homebound persons can check on one another.

As article writers. Every publication can use additional writers. Homebound people may be invited to write for the church newsletter. Those with good telephone skills can conduct interviews to gather information. Others may want to provide devotional material. Still others can provide the valuable service of proofreading.

As good-will ambassadors. Homebound people can be excellent encouragers. Most have access to telephones and many to e-mail. As they learn of celebrative events in the church and community, they can offer congratulations. Their acknowledgment of births, graduations, job promotions, milestones, engagements, and weddings will be appreciated.

Appreciate Leaders

Plan a Dedication Sunday

Set aside one Sunday each year to honor each member's ministry outside the church building. Acknowledging the way people are living their faith outside the church strengthens their leadership inside the church.

Once a year, usually on Labor Day Sunday, New Hope Church invites members to come to worship wearing the clothes they wear in their work, whether that be at home, in volunteer service, or in their places of employment. Although some people dress similarly for work and church, the congregation will be visually impacted as they gather and see their brothers and sisters in hospital scrubs, postal service uniforms, mechanic uniforms, dress-for-success business suits, and sweats. The pastor says it gives the congregation an "aha moment" as they see the graphic illustration of how their church reaches into the community.

One year the dedication service focused on "hands" as the representation of work. The theme was "Use These Hands, Lord." The theme Scripture was Psalm 90:17. Songs included Frances R. Havergal's traditional hymn "Take My Life and Let It Be Consecrated, Lord, to Thee," an anonymously written gospel song titled "Do All the Good You Can," and the praise chorus by Bob Kilpatrick "Lord, Be Glorified." The familiar poem "God Has No Hands but Our Hands" by Annie Johnson Flint was also incorporated into the service of worship.

Mark Leadership Transitions

At the beginning of the church year, incorporate a commissioning service into the worship hour. Too often people are elected at a business meeting and quietly begin their term of office largely unsupported by the rest of the congregation. Commissioning new leaders authenticates the work they do and adds visibility.

At the close of their term, some leaders are ready to disappear quietly. But what message do we communicate when we let them go without a word? Moderators and presidents may receive appropriate recognition, but let's not forget the board and committee members who have served with them. At the very least, outgoing leaders should be recognized within the group where they have been serving. The larger church family should also be given the opportunity to thank them.

Express Appreciation

Just as the congregation participates in "Clergy Appreciation Sunday," pastors do well to show appreciation for the work of the laity. Pastors who see themselves as CEOs who want laity to perform as staff often engender indifference and suspicion. Clergy who are servant leaders attract laity.

When a work team shows up to trim the shrubs on the church property, let the congregation know who is responsible for the great job. If the order of worship doesn't lend itself to this type of informality, a printed note of appreciation in the bulletin or newsletter is effective. In fact, a piece of paper can say a lot. Consider printing certificates of appreciation to hand out from time to time. And don't forget the faithful volunteers who work behind the scenes: Joe and Francis who arrive early to make the coffee, Phil who updates the church sign weekly, and Sharon who folds the bulletins every Friday.

A brunch or lunch to honor leaders communicates appreciation. So that no one has to spend hours in preparation, have the meal catered. Or perhaps your church has one of those volunteers who loves to cook for special events like this. It can be as simple or elaborate as you want to make it, but above all, the event should shout, "Thank you!" Speeches and special presentations may or may not be in order. If your church's tradition doesn't dictate the plan, consider a program of light entertainment that just says "enjoy."

● ● ●

Engaging laity takes work. Leadership skills need to be honed. Dormant abilities need to be awakened. Identification and cultivation of leaders is an ongoing, intentional process. When it becomes part of the root system of a church, both the corporate body and the individuals within it benefit.

Notes

1. Richard Sutton, Tomorrow's Harvest Workshop, First Baptist Church, Storm Lake, IA, October 19, 2002.

2. "Mission and Vision," Prairie Baptist Church, Shawnee Mission, KS, http://prairiebaptist.org/about/mission-statement/ (accessed February 12, 2011).

3. Richard Sutton and Harry Riggs, *Good Soil* (National Ministries, Small Church Team, 1998).

4. George A. Butterick, ed., *The Interpreter's Dictionary of the Bible*, vol. 3, s.v. "Luke" (Nashville: Abingdon, 1962), 180.

5. Forrest Carter, *The Education of Little Tree* (Albuquerque: University of New Mexico Press, 1986), 57.

The Leaders among Us

Big churches, little churches, and those in between all across the country are recognizing that the criteria for determining the success of a church are not the same as for a business or even for many nonprofit organizations. The worldly, materialistic criteria embraced by others are not what it takes to become the body of Christ.

Churches come to life when they reject defeat and instead claim the joy of being faithful. They come to life when they stop using external judgments that demean them. New energy comes forth when churches selflessly serve the least, the lonely, and the locked out—not for what the church will get out of it but simply because of the joy that Christ has put deep in their hearts.

In tens of thousands of churches, acts of love and caring are renewing the faithful and inspiring a new crop of leaders. Seeking to be the hands and feet of Jesus is bringing a rebirth of purpose. But not one of these churches is perfect any more than any one individual Christian is perfect. Each Christian and each church walks through storms and sunshine. Sometimes we measure up to our own expectations, and sometimes we don't. The challenge is to accept that reality and move on! The church thrives when it is a place of meaningful affirmation and joyous courage.

Where have all the leaders gone? They're in your church. They are the people in the pew. If, as some say, "there is a little leader in each of us," the church can help congregants uncover their inner leader.

Clergy are on the front lines of this endeavor. Pastors minister with leaders and followers and spend quality time with both. They receive strength from those "born leaders" and give strength to the congregants who seek to develop their "inner leader." They till the soil, add nutrients, plant the seeds, and tend the seedlings.

As people in the pew develop their competencies as leaders and use what they learn, the congregation celebrates a harvest. New leaders step into place. Other leaders assume the role of followers. But the work is never complete. The process of identifying and cultivating leaders is ongoing. Recall God's promise to Noah:

> "As long as the earth endures,
> > seedtime and harvest, cold and heat,
> > summer and winter, day and night,
> > > shall not cease." (Genesis 8:22, NRSV)

Avid gardeners eagerly anticipate the midwinter arrival of seed catalogs. Regardless of whether the previous growing season produced a bumper crop, they're ready to begin again. About two months before the last normal spring frost, they start the seeds in good soil indoors. They make sure the seeds have the right amount of light and water, and they joyfully watch the seeds spring to life. When the seedlings are two to three inches tall, gardeners transplant them into larger containers, using the same good soil mix they provided the dormant seeds. When the earth begins to warm, gardeners are out there turning over the soil and adding the necessary nutrients. Before planting the seedlings in the ground, gardeners know to gradually expose them to the sun's rays. When the time is right, the seedlings are placed in the ground to be tended and cultivated in the months ahead. And once again gardeners celebrate a time of harvest.

So it is in the church. Building a leadership team that will help your church's ministry thrive is time-consuming and unending, but investing in the cultivation of current and potential leaders pays off. The stories you have read in this book are just a few examples of the successes churches may enjoy. Tap the root; engage and empower the laity, and write your own success story.

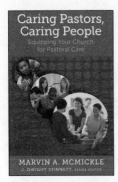

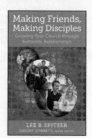

Praise for *Making Friends,*
Making Disciples: Growing Your Church
through Authentic Relationships

"Lee Spitzer sees friendship as a necessary good in and of itself, a virtue and practice that constitutes humanness, validates personhood, and creates community... Establishing friendships within significant circles of love and becoming a friend of God are the first two steps in seeing our faith communities grow and thrive in authentic relationship and mission."

—David W Augsburger, Professor of Pastoral Care and Counseling,
Fuller Theological Seminary, Pasadena, CA

"Lee Spitzer not only shows how good friendships enrich our lives, but also how they bless the church by nurturing Christians for faithful discipleship and mission. In chapters that explore Jesus' model of friendship, friendship as a spiritual journey, and the different kinds of friendship, Spitzer insightfully portrays why good friendships help make the church and our world a better place. *Making Friends, Making Disciples* reminds us that friendships are both a grace and a calling."

—Paul J. Wadell, Professor of Religious Studies, St. Norbert College,
De Pere, Wisconsin; author, *Becoming Friends:*
Worship, Justice and the Practice of Christian Friendship

"Lee gets to the heart of the matter, asserting that the church is a Christ-centered community of friends that is committed to making more friends. His approach goes much deeper than 'friendship evangelism.' Lee explores 'how friendship informs the internal life (discipleship) and outreach ministry (evangelism in a holistic sense) of the church in the twenty-first century.' He argues powerfully that cultivating friendship with God and neighbor is a spiritual discipline, not having some ulterior motive, but because God has called us to make and be friends."

—Rev. Dr. J. Dwight Stinnett, Living Church Series Editor; Executive
Minister, American Baptist Churches, Great Rivers Region

"This easy-to-read guide flows in a conversational style and enlightens the topic that's dear to most believers' hearts: deepening friendships. Recommended for church leaders, Sunday school teachers, small group leaders, and book clubs." —*Church Libraries*, Winter 2010-11